The Five-Dollar Gold Piece

THE DEVELOPMENT OF A POINT OF VIEW

The Five-Dollar Gold Piece

Gold Piece

THE DEVELOPMENT OF A POINT OF VIEW

BY *Orville Prescott*

ILLUSTRATED BY VASILIU

RANDOM HOUSE • NEW YORK

TO LILIAS, OF COURSE

NOTE: I have given imaginary names to more than a dozen people, to three schools and to one town. I have also changed the appearance and the past record of several persons. To this extent, and only to this extent, this book contains a trace of fiction. Everything else is as true as can be expected in an autobiography written from memory by a man who never kept a diary.

The following people generously gave of their time and effort to help me get this book written: Miss Elizabeth Schenck of the Lee Keedick lecture bureau, who tracked down for me some elusive statistics about the lecture business; Miss Ruth Peet Smith, my mother's cousin, who answered my plea for anecdotes about my maternal grandfather; Mr. and Mrs. Kenneth Eves, who patiently read every page and pointed out many a rough patch where more sandpaper was needed; my father, O. W. Prescott, who supplied material, corrected errors where my memory strayed and encouraged me to go on writing as he has done all my life; and my wife, who shared my struggles to the extent that she was almost a collaborator.

· introduction ·

When I was six years old my Grandmother Sherwin offered me a five-dollar gold piece if I would learn to read. I had no notion what a five-dollar gold piece was, but it was evidently desirable and I knew that I would have to learn soon, anyway. A few days later I read her three pages in big type from my first-grade primer about Douglas, the Scots hero. What became of the gold piece I do not know, but occasionally I grieve for it. It marked the most important turning point of my life. Ever since that summer afternoon when I stood at Amma's knee in the drawing room of "The Big House" and proved that I could read, the reading of books has been my principal interest in life; and for many years reading books and writing about them has been my occupation.

This dominating interest I share with many thousands of bookish people. We all have something important in common, but often not much else. Our genes and glands are different, and so are our experiences of life and our ideas based upon them. To what extent our ideas are the result of deliberate thought, to what they are the inevitable result of our characters and the influences which shaped

them, no one can tell. But modern psychologists agree about the importance of the twig's early bendings. I believe, rightly or wrongly, that ever since I learned to read, my twig has bent noticeably to the pressure of books as well as to that of people and circumstances.

In the following pages I have written about the impact of some of those books, people and circumstances upon my thought and about some of the ideas and opinions which I consequently hold. On the whole, my life has been fortunate, and since I have small use for writers who beat their breasts and bare their sins in public, there are no startling revelations in these pages. But there is an insistent urge in many writers to record that this is what I saw and part of this I was, and that this I do believe. This book is the result of my surrendering to that urge.

The Five-Dollar Gold Piece

THE DEVELOPMENT OF A POINT OF VIEW

· one ·

I have more relations than I can keep track of and far more than I have ever known personally. Since James Prescott settled in Hampton, New Hampshire, in 1665 the Prescotts have multiplied exceedingly. But I do not know as much as I should about my ancestors and for many years I did not care to know about them. I now realize that this was a mistake. When I was young I did not understand how interesting elderly relations could be, let alone remote ancestors. And my memory has failed to retain much of what I once knew about my relatives— to my present regret. This, I believe, is a typically American attitude, at least it is in the present century. Every generation feels new and daring and is so excited by pressing current problems that it is indifferent to the past (except, of course, in parts of New England and in the South). Each individual feels that he must hoe his own row and plant his own crop, often in fields a thousand miles from those his father tilled. Families do not stay put. Children scatter and the old are left alone.

When my Grandfather Prescott was a boy on his father's farm in Maine his ambition was to be a schoolteacher.

He became one while still in his teens, but soon discovered that his restless, ambitious spirit was too confined in a one-room country school. His father, a respected but hardly prosperous farmer, understood Grandfather's decision to seek his fortune in the West, but he was not in a position to give his son much material aid. Grandfather started West with his father's blessing, a Bible and a team of oxen. In Pennsylvania he went into the lumber business, and as his fortunes prospered he acquired his own tracts of timber and rafted his logs down the Allegheny River to Pittsburgh. After many years of successful operations in Pennsylvania, Grandfather transferred his logging business to the Saginaw Bay area of Michigan. To dispose of his own product he opened a lumber yard in Cleveland and there he settled down and made his permanent home.

Charles Holden Prescott was a Yankee trader who knew all there was to know about lumber, from the virgin forest to the planks and two-by-fours he sold to building contractors. But Grandfather was not a conventional businessman. He was also an ordained Baptist minister. To me as a small child he was a remote figure of awful dignity, massive, handsome, white-haired, smooth-shaven except for a ruff of soft white hairs under his chin. He used to sit in a large chair at one end of his living room in his fine house on East 55th Street in Cleveland on Sunday afternoons and hold court among his sons and daughters, in-laws and grandchildren. Not until long after his death in 1913 at the age of eighty-four, when I was six, did I learn what a man Grandfather was.

He was a man who inspired legends. That some of them were false I learned with sorrow when I asked my father about several stories which I had cherished. But the bare bones of truth include Grandfather's enormous physical energy, his pleasure in keeping many irons in the fire, and his religious zeal. Although he never held a pastorate, he preached frequently and his idea of a vacation was to conduct a revival meeting. He used to preach to the lumberjacks in his own camps, and at the conclusion of his sermon, challenge any one of them to a game of checkers or a wrestling match. According to family tradition, the lumberjacks seldom won at either. No matter what his text, he always preached the same sermon—a rousing exposition of fundamental Baptist doctrine. He often baptized people in nearby rivers in the depths of winter and he always insisted that neither he nor any of his converts ever caught a cold. He was known as "the businessman preacher" and rejoiced in the title.

In his Pennsylvania days Grandfather's various business interests required that he be away from his home on frequent trips, which he made on horseback. When he came home Grandmother often had to report that the children had misbehaved. To restore proper discipline Grandfather would order them to fall in line, like soldiers, and would drill them in squads right and left and other dress maneuvers.

In addition to his lumber business Grandfather operated general stores in Pennsylvania and in Michigan and, as a farmer's son, he always felt a need to have a farm of his own. He had them in Pennsylvania, Michigan and Ohio. A devout and honorable man, Grandfather was also a rugged nineteenth-century individualist who liked his own way and knew how to get it. In his early days in Michigan, a narrow-gauge railroad hauled Grandfather's logs for some twenty miles to his mill and Grandfather was convinced that he was being charged too high a freight rate. He could do nothing about it, however, until the railroad went into receivership and was sold at public auction. Grandfather bought the railroad and, although he had no experience in railroading, succeeded in operating it efficiently. Some years later when he sold his little railroad to the Detroit and Mackinac Railway at a pleasant profit, he made sure that he would pay what he considered a satisfactory rate for hauling his logs; he also insisted in the terms of sale that any train he flagged at any time would stop and pick him up.

Compared with Grandfather's striking personality, Grandmother's must have been gentle and unobtrusive. My father, who was their seventh child and fourth son, has told me stories about his father, but has rarely mentioned his mother. To me Grandmother is only a faint memory, a white-haired old lady in a black shawl who used to take her grandchildren to a dark closet where she kept oranges, then considered a rare treat.

Far clearer in my memory is my great-uncle, Elisha. There was a man no child could forget. His hair was white and scanty, his back was bowed, most of his teeth were missing. The useless and shiftless elder brother, Grandfather had always had to support him. At various times Uncle Elisha clerked in Grandfather's stores, but he always preferred reading a newspaper to waiting on customers. Unconcerned about business, a happy bachelor, a kindly putterer who liked to raise vegetables and chickens, Uncle Elisha lacked his brother's religious zeal. Every Sunday he went to church and every Sunday he went to sleep a few minutes after the minister began his sermon. "Fortunately," says my father, "he did not snore, so we never bothered to waken him. When we asked him why he was not interested enough in the sermon to stay awake, he always replied that he listened long enough to see that the minister started out all right, and then, since he did not have to worry any more about it, he preferred to go to sleep."

Uncle Elisha was a storyteller. On Sunday afternoons when the clan gathered, after the children had spoken politely to Grandfather and Grandmother, Uncle Elisha would entertain us in the little back room. He would spin long yarns about bears and panthers and Indians and hair-raising adventures. They are blurred in my memory now and I cannot recall whether he pretended to have played an heroic part in his own stories. But the picture of six or eight children seated on the arms of his chair and on the floor around him is still clear in my mind.

My mother's father was also a New Englander. Grandfather Sherwin was born on a farm near Springfield, Vermont. At thirteen he went to work in the local general store, sleeping under the counter at night. While still in his teens he tramped around the state taking daguerreotype pictures. But when the lure of richer lands and growing towns in the Middle West precipitated a general exodus of ambitious young men from northern New England, Grandfather Sherwin went, too. In Cleveland his tenacity of purpose, his gentlemanly dignity which inspired trust and respect, and his acute business sense made him a financial success. He was the founder and, until his death, the president of the Sherwin Williams Paint Company.

One of my Grandfather Sherwin's fellow members of the First Baptist Church, an older and considerably more successful businessman, used to escort the girl who became my grandmother home from Wednesday night prayer meetings. His name was John D. Rockefeller. But no romantic attachment developed from that acquaintance, and Frances Smith married Henry Alden Sherwin. They had four children, a son who died young and three daughters of whom my mother, the youngest, was the only one to marry.

Many years after his own marriage Grandfather Sherwin's nephew came to him for advice. He was in love and wanted to marry, but wasn't sure that he could afford it. "Don't marry until you have an annual income of five thousand dollars; I didn't," said Grandfather. Considering how large an income that was in the 1860's when he married, this bit of super-cautious advice is a revealing indication of Grandfather's careful, methodical approach to life.

Grandfather Sherwin was short, slight, trim, unassumingly good-looking. He wore a mustache which drooped part way over his upper lip, but which never achieved the luxuriance of many of its contemporaries. Always polite, considerate and kind, Grandfather Sherwin had an unusual gift for silence. Outside of his business his principal interests were the Baptist church, fishing, collecting books on angling and books by and about Isaak Walton, and improving the farm he owned near Kirtland, Ohio.

Grandmother Sherwin was a tiny woman with features of a cameo-like delicacy, a sweet expression and a mass of beautiful white hair. I remember her as always calm and dignified, either sitting reading in her favorite chair in "the morning room" or presiding over the tea table on the big verandah at Winden. Amma inspired affection and respect in all who knew her, but she was somewhat overshadowed by the grave distinction of her husband and by the forceful personality of her eldest daughter.

My Aunt Belle Sherwin, called Boo by her niece and nephews, was a remarkable woman. Born in 1868, from her childhood she behaved like a character in a play by George Bernard Shaw, to the baffled bewilderment and reluctant admiration of her parents. Boo was a determined intellectual, an emancipated champion of worthy causes, a fighter for women's rights, a woman of tireless energy, great intellectual capacity and absolutely no sense of humor. She insisted on going to college at a time when few girls went to college, and graduated from Wellesley in the class of 1889. That was difficult enough for my grandparents to accept. But Boo was not satisfied. She then insisted on studying history at Oxford, when the number of American girls who studied in European universities could be counted on a few hands.

On her return to the United States she became a teacher of history, but found her energies too great and her interests too various for the quiet backwater of teaching in girls' schools. Boo went into social work, organized classes and nurseries in Cleveland's Italian slums, and inspired a devotion among her pupils which lasted as long as she lived. But the suffragette movement and votes for women called, and Boo became one of its national leaders. She also signalized her independence by becoming an Episcopalian and a Democrat. She served in the Ohio state administration of Governor James M. Cox and, after women's votes were won, Boo was one of the founders and organizers of The League of Women Voters, serving as its national president for ten years.

Boo was a natural executive and always took command of any situation. Her career brought her into contact with many people and she made many abiding friendships. These mystified me when I was young, because Boo was tactless and managing to the point of being domineering. However, I discovered as I grew older that Boo's kindness, her generosity and her fierce loyalty to her friends more than atoned for her often prickly personality. And since she was highly intelligent, her conversation was likely to be thoroughly interesting in its solemn way. Conversation with Boo was always on her own terms. She was used to command. She had always been able to do anything she wanted and to have anything she wanted. When Boo was in her old age, I used to feel that a call on her was rather like being granted an audience by a vigorous and intellectual Queen Victoria.

Once when Boo was nearly eighty I was astonished and delighted to hear her say, "Oh, no, she's not married. She's an *intelligent* woman." Without any sign of noticing how controversial or how revealing a remark she had just made, she continued her conversation and my mind wandered. How representative, I wondered, was this expression of an obviously minority opinion? Did many members of Boo's new breed of women hold it? Florence Nightingale might well have felt the same way, since she was one of the first, as well as the most celebrated, of the crusading, managing, organizing women who have done so much good in the modern world and have swept so much dust out of so many dark corners.

But most of the world's famous unmarried women, I decided, from Elizabeth I on, would have disagreed with my distinguished aunt. Most of them, I feel sure, would agree with Mrs. Robert Henrey, who said in her charming book, *Madeleine Grown Up: The Autobiography of a French Girl*, "Our whole business is getting ourselves loved." I have strayed a little from the straight path of memory, as

I expect to do often in these informal pages. Now it is time to straighten my course.

Today it is generally considered a literary asset to have had eccentric parents. Hesketh Pearson, the English biographer, has remarked that few children are so unlucky as not to have had one comical parent. In that foolish sense I was unlucky in my parents, but in no other. They were neither eccentric nor comical. On the contrary. My father has a delightful sense of humor and can be extremely funny when he chooses; but anything eccentric, raffish or crudely comical would be as foreign to his nature as it was to my mother's. Highly conventional by instinct, they were also conventional by conviction. Good manners and a decent respect for the opinions of mankind required a certain amount of seemly decorum in the world in which they always lived. Cultivated but not intellectual, kind, responsible, they were typical members of the prosperous society of Cleveland, the easternmost of the Middle West's large cities.

They gave their children the usual privileges, dancing, riding and music lessons; sent them to private schools and to college; watched them grow up in the war-torn teens and frenzied twenties with solicitude and some alarm about the new notions and social changes which were transforming theirs and their children's world; and they never sought to establish an intimacy of relationship which would have been as embarrassing to them as to their children. Consequently, we led a sheltered life, but an intellectually independent one. My father was too busy selling lumber for the family company and on weekends too busy playing tennis when he was young and golf when he was older to discuss manners or morals or ideas with his children. Besides, I doubt if it would have occurred to him to do so. He knew that we knew he expected us to behave like gentlemen and to honor the sound business principles of the Republican party, and that was that.

My mother was serene, patient, gentle, utterly lacking my father's sociability, content to read rapidly but uncritically, to be present with her affection and understanding when any child should need her, but rather proud of her common-sense attitude and lack of sentimental foolishness. She could have put on many of the airs of a grand lady if she had cared to; she didn't care to. It wasn't until late in her life when she was stricken with a prolonged and painful illness that her children, who had always loved her devotedly, realized how great were her courage and her gallantry of spirit.

The house in which I was born no longer stands. The quiet, tree-lined street on which it stood is now occupied by garages, third-rate shops and sleazy boarding houses. When we lived there in the early years of the twentieth century it was still a typically nineteenth-century residential street. I used to watch the lamplighter each evening, just like the child in Stevenson's poem. And the scissors grinder who rang a bell to herald his coming was a sinister figure. The children on the block "knew" that he was a kidnapper and must be fled from with delicious terror (a childish echo of the famous Charlie Ross disappearance?).

When the first airplane appeared in the sky we all rushed out into the street to stare at the marvel. We used to stare at automobiles, too, which were also marvels. The first car owned by a member of the family was Mother's electric, a high, square, elegant vehicle with a cut-glass vase for flowers and a long steering bar which Mother gripped with frozen attention. But some time before the appearance of the electric, the lumber company acquired one of the early Wintons. Grandfather Prescott's coachman, transformed into a chauffeur, drove it, picking up my Uncle Charles, then my father and then my Uncle Howard to take them to their office on the flats of the Cuyahoga River under the shadow of the viaduct.

Around the corner from our house on Euclid Avenue was Grandfather Sherwin's house, a large, square red-brick building with a cupola on top and an iron deer in the front yard—·as was only fitting for a house in what was then called millionaires' row. But we moved to a big new house on the Heights just after my seventh birthday in 1913, and my Sherwin grandparents sold their house in order to spend most of the year at Winden, their country estate always called "The Farm," and rented an apartment for the winter months. So those old houses are only dim shadows. Life really began when we moved, and all my childhood which counts is associated with the Heights or Winden. We, too, spent our summers at Winden in a cluster of frame cottages Mother insisted on calling "The Camp," although no one else ever used the term.

Winden was wonderful, a 200-acre farm in Kirtland, Ohio, some twenty miles east of Cleveland. It was a working farm with cows and horses and sheep and poultry, orchards and pastures, fields of wheat, oats, alfalfa and corn. Grandfather Sherwin employed a superintendent, a dairyman and a number of farm hands and gardeners to operate it. But his ideas for improvements kept altering its character, making it less and less like a working farm and more and more like a country estate.

He built an aviary where he kept golden pheasants. He installed rustic benches and bridges at convenient locations. He built a new and handsome gate and a new driveway which swept up to the Big House in graceful curves.

All of these changes, and the elaborate garden which he did not live to see completed, were expressions of his abiding love of beauty. Usually he did not put his feelings into words, but once as he stood on the verandah at Winden and looked across his own acres and the serene valley of the east branch of the Chagrin River to the Kirtland hills, where a white church spire gleamed, he exclaimed to his niece, "Ruth, heaven couldn't be any more beautiful than this!" To keep it that way he saw to it that the church was painted annually at his own expense.

The garden was laid out on a gently sloping hillside which had formerly been an apple orchard. In a series of descending terraces connected by stone staircases were alternating fountains and pools, a grotto and a long arbor, all of them surrounded by flower beds and those on the highest level backed by walls of massive masonry. It was very beautiful. Today, when death and taxes have wrought their usual havoc, it is a melancholy experience to walk through the tangled desolation where once was so much beauty. It would be less emotionally disturbing not to return to the willow pool and the terraces where the iris and larkspur, the roses and thyme once bloomed. But something draws me back, and whenever I return to Cleveland I usually find myself brooding once again in the forsaken garden at Winden.

The Big House was so called to distinguish it from the Prescott family cottages a half-mile away. It was a large rambling structure of red brick, white trim and enormous white verandahs. At one end was an imposing wing, the fireproof library built at a later date to house Grandfather Sherwin's angling collection.

Summers at Winden in many respects were idyllic. We had a whole farm to roam, a muddy river to swim in and later a swimming pool, a tennis court and only a minimum of token chores assigned for character-building purposes. But I wonder what a modern authority on child psychology would think of them. My brothers were six and four-and-a-half years older than I, much too big to be my companions, although they did take me with them to the swimming hole and saw that I did not drown. My sister was twenty months younger and only a girl, a lovable child lost in a private dream world of her own populated by paper dolls and other mysterious feminine concerns. Except when my cousin Barnard was invited to visit me, I had no one to play with, no companion, no competition. And I did not know that I lacked them; for I had discovered the joy of reading.

Shortly after my gold-piece triumph my mother asked me what I wanted for my seventh birthday. Charmed with my newly acquired reading skill, probably influenced by the rows of handsomely bound sets in the Big House library, I asked for a set of books, not a particular set, any set would do. Mother responded by giving me the first three volumes of Thornton W. Burgess' animal stories for children. The adventures of Johnny Chuck, Jimmy Skunk and Peter Rabbit delighted me and lured me on to other better written, more realistic animal stories. For several years I lived imaginatively in an animal world, devouring the complete works of Ernest Thompson Seton, Clarence Hawks, Charles G. D. Roberts and others, learning a great deal of animal lore in the process but all of it entirely theoretical.

I could recognize any animal's tracks if they were drawn in a book. But I had considerable difficulty identifying real tracks in the snow of the ravine between the Shaker lakes a few blocks from our Fairmount Boulevard home. Once my cousin Barnard and I found the tracks of a tiger in the ravine and on another occasion tracks which could only have been those of a gorilla, which was considerably more than Daniel Boone could have done in a patch of woods three miles from the city limits of Cleveland, Ohio.

Fortunately for me, in view of my summer isolation, was the fact that my Uncle Howard's house was next door to ours and that Barnard shared my enthusiasm for animals. We read the same books about animals, went tracking together on Saturdays and Sundays, and were partners in several commercial projects. The first of these was a flier in the crayfish business. We captured several dozen, took them to school in a large mason jar full of water, found sales disappointingly slow, and left the jar in my gymnasium locker, forgetting all about it. A week later a frightful odor made the gym almost uninhabitable. Barnard and I were just as curious as any of the teachers or boys as to the mysterious cause. When the stench was tracked down to our dead and decomposing crayfish, we were as surprised as anybody and much more upset. They seemed to think that we had caused that smell on purpose!

Not counting several puppies presented to me by Mrs. Schoenfeldt, our German laundress, and Sandy, a mongrel who never learned anything except how much I loved him and unscrupulously took advantage of the fact, the first really important animals in my life were Belgian hares. Barnard acquired several of these and took me into partnership in the rabbit-breeding business. We painted a large sign and nailed it to a tree in front of Uncle Howard's handsome Georgian house. "Prescott Rabbitry" it blazoned in letters three times as large as those of the only other sign, which said, "3097 No Deliveries."

Belgian hares are not like Easter bunnies. They are

much larger and they are temperamental. Henrietta was so temperamental I never dared feed her without first putting on a pair of heavy leather gloves. A cross between a wolf and a she-devil, she could bite to the bone. Uncle Howard never appreciated Henrietta until one Sunday morning, when he joined us in the loft over his garage, which was the Prescott Rabbitry's place of business. The time had come when Henrietta was to be introduced to the prospective father of her children, and Uncle Howard thought it only fitting and proper that Barnard and I be shooed outside while he officiated.

We waited for a summons to return, which never came. Finally we knocked timidly and reentered our own domain. Henrietta did not exactly have Uncle Howard cowering in a corner, but her bared fangs and fiery glare certainly did have him thoroughly subdued. We had to tend to matters ourselves and demonstrate the correct technique. Uncle Howard should have known better than to try to move Henrietta into the male's cage. We calmly put the male into Henrietta's and all was well.

Your true animal lover is never content with the animals he owns. He always wants more. The natural increase of the hares was insufficient for Barnard's and my enthusiasm. We bought more. We bought other animals, too. Soon the rabbitry housed two guinea pig ancestors and their numerous descendants, one white rabbit, two Flemish Giant rabbits, four mourning doves, five chickens, six white rats and a dozen Japanese waltzing mice. The peak population according to the last official census was forty-one. It seemed as if we had a bear by the tail and could not let go. Bales of hay and grain were rapidly consumed. Every morning before breakfast, every afternoon after school, all day Saturday and Sunday we fed, watered, bred, sorted and cleaned cages. We waited on those animals hand and foot. No customers appeared even to "browse" among our livestock. Our business went ever more deeply into the red. We had to drown the rats, at least Barnard did, for although I loathed them I was too soft-hearted to kill them. For that matter, I was so soft-hearted I always made a point of stepping over worms and ants, to the amazement of more thick-skinned friends.

Left to our own devices we might have completely disappeared beneath a flood of hopping, crawling, scuttering, squeaking creatures. Luckily, Barnard was sent away to preparatory school. The rabbitry was clearly too much for me to handle single-handed. Uncle Howard and my father, with the mysterious methods of grown-ups, stepped in and scattered our flocks and herds to what remote regions I never knew.

For unknown reasons my parents did not send me to the school my elder brothers had attended. Theirs was large and conventional. Mine was small and experimental. In those days progressive education with its fetishes of "learning by doing," "self-expression" and lack of discipline had not yet become an international vogue. But my school was experimental in its own way and its experiments reflected the ideas of its founder and headmaster. It was his theory that children needed character development more than formal education, and character development was a matter of intensive, personal inspiration.

The classes were small. We were subjected to "habit-forming drills," forced to listen to continual high-minded exhortations about fair play and honor, taken to see pictures in the art museum and to a touring production of *Hamlet*. No serious harm would have been done by this if all the teachers had been as able as the English teacher,

John J. Carney, who won my devotion and admiration. But several of the others were incompetent. They did not make us work and they did not hold us to a standard. I doubt if the headmaster was aware of this. The results, for me, were disastrous.

Although the school had put no pressure upon me and had not told either my parents or me that I was doing badly, when the time came for me to take entrance examinations to the preparatory school my parents had chosen I failed dismally and was put back a class. This humiliating situation probably would not have arisen if my class at the Cleveland school had not been the first to reach preparatory school age. This came about because the school was new and grew through a new first grade each year and promotion of the others. So my class was always the top class. There were never any boys in school older than we were. The teachers never had to think about the scholarship levels maintained by other schools until my class finished the ninth grade. It was a ridiculous system.

Worse still was the fact that there were only seven boys in my class. Year after year we lorded it over the younger boys and became so intimately acquainted with each other that the atmosphere was wonderfully warm and cozy. No competition to speak of! No bigger, tougher boys to beware of! No large group to adjust to! Instead of building character as the headmaster dreamed he was doing, he was delaying the development of character, making sure that once we left his pampered nursery, life would be much more difficult than it need have been.

Coasting along in a pleasant daze, with all my real interest concentrated on the books I read in my too abundant spare time, learning little French and less mathematics, spelling atrociously, I occasionally had a fleeting suspicion that all was not well. My parents, who thought that I must be bright because of the unusual number of books I read, had their doubts, too, but only infrequently, whenever they noticed that I could not do problems about two men rowing at different speeds toward each other on a river with a current of such and such; or when they wondered why I spelled the same word so many ways. But neither they nor I really worried seriously. The school was so fine, so idealistic, and such nice boys went there!

Like many bookish children, I was a poor performer in the school gym and on the athletic field, and I didn't much care. The occasional ridicule I suffered because of a dropped fly or a crucial strike-out was good-natured. And, anyway, I had more important things on my mind. The same indifference to the unavoidable nuisances of life made my five years of piano lessons a dismal failure. My mother had no ear for music. As long as she heard noise from the piano she assumed that practicing was being done. I remember playing the scale of C continuously through many an hour's practice while I read a book propped on the music rack. An exasperating child!

Some children are so engrossed with sports and games and tools and all the intensely active life of childhood that they have no interest in books. Others can take them or leave them alone. But I lived in books. They seemed more important and interesting than anything in real life. At first I read, entirely uncritically, anything which fell into my hands, the more romantic and exciting the better. With equal joy I read the western novels of Zane Grey, the Fu Manchu thrillers of Sax Rohmer, the Tarzan books, bound volumes of *St. Nicholas*, and the historical romances of Winston Churchill. Mother sometimes objected mildly when she found me deep in a forbidden Arsène

Lupin mystery; but she could not bring herself to make much of an issue of it because more frequently I would be reading *Ben Hur,* or *The Last Days of Pompeii,* or *Uncle Tom's Cabin,* or *Treasure Island* and other classics approved for children. Our house was always full of books and there were more in the Big House at Winden.

At Winden there were several key associations which opened alluring vistas into the American past. Every summer during the hot, dry days of August we would hear the bells. Golfers missing a putt on the nearby course might mutter savagely, farmers in their fields might not even lift their heads to listen to the familiar sound; but to me the mellow tolling meant a deliciously close contact with something mysterious, bizarre and sinister, for the bells were not ordinary church bells. They were the bells of the Mormon Temple at Kirtland, Ohio, calling to worship the faithful followers of one of the heretical sects of the Church of Jesus Christ of Latter-day Saints.

I used to sit on the stile over the fence between the corn field and the cow pasture and look across the green valley of the east branch of the Chagrin River and see the white spire of the temple, where I knew that Joseph Smith had once preached and where Brigham Young himself and the murderous Porter Rockwell had once worshipped. In that very river in which I learned to swim, legend had it that Smith had walked upon the water, aided by a submerged plank. And weren't the Mormons polygamous and hadn't Conan Doyle and Robert Louis Stevenson written the most gruesomely thrilling stories about them?

It was at Winden that the Civil War jumped out of books and into the world of direct experience. My Grandmother Sherwin's brother Frank used to come and visit and find little to keep him occupied in his brother-in-law's big house. With time on his hands he welcomed my questions. I asked many, for Uncle Frank had fought in the ranks at Shiloh and Chickamauga. I remember asking him if a soldier in battle aimed at a particular enemy soldier or just shot at the enemy line. Uncle Frank, a little man with a large white mustache, thought that over for a long pause and then admitted that it was best to aim at a particular enemy, but that usually he was so excited and frightened he just shot in the general direction and hoped for the best.

Uncle Frank was captured and spent more than a year as a prisoner in the infamous prison camp at Andersonville, Georgia. He had long since lost any bitterness he once felt, but he seemed to enjoy describing the horrors of life in Andersonville: the foul mush shoveled off mule carts which was the prisoners' principal food, the many men who died of malaria and dysentery; the guards who shot any prisoner who even stretched a hand beyond a rope strung three feet inside the palisade which surrounded the camp.

One summer when Uncle Frank came to Winden he brought a large package under his arm. It was a present for me. While my grandparents, my parents, my aunts, my brothers and my sister watched, I unwrapped it. Neatly framed in cheap gilt was a large oil painting of Andersonville prison painted by himself. In crude and brilliant colors, with faulty perspective and clumsy amateur draftsmanship, Uncle Frank had painted everything he remembered, the gaunt, bearded, half-starved men in miserable rags, the mush cart, the dirty tents and even a prisoner stretching under the rope for a crust of bread and being shot by the guard. For several years Uncle Frank's painting hung on the wall of my bedroom in the Winden cottage; but finally Mother could stand the ugly thing no longer and banished it.

Another visitor to Winden looked upon the Civil War from a rather different point of view. Cousin Ida was a plump, elderly old maid, the daughter of my Grandfather Prescott's first cousin, a doctor who had gone South and established a practice at Staunton in the Shenandoah Valley of Virginia. Although a Northerner by birth, the doctor had served as an army surgeon with Stonewall Jackson's foot cavalry. Cousin Ida had lived most of her life in the North, but her childhood memories of the war were vivid and her allegiance to the Confederacy was unshaken. Her tales about the vandalism and looting of Sherman's troops, which she had seen with her own eyes, were grisly.

I remember asking her if now that it was all so long ago wasn't she glad that the North had won and the Union had been preserved. With pursed lips and flashing eye, snapping off a thread with which she was darning a pair of my stockings, she replied, "When two people can't agree it's better for them to separate." I could almost hear the rebel yell.

My third Winden contact with the Civil War was Gibson. Gibson was a tall, lean, morose and silent Negro who had been a slave in Alabama. His hair was white, his skin was shiny black, he never spoke to a small boy, and he was said to do no more work than was absolutely necessary. When the wolf got too far into the doorway he would work for Grandfather Sherwin, but he refused to work regularly. I used to stare at Gibson with fascination. There in the flesh was a former slave, one of the men Uncle Frank had fought to free, one of the causes of the Civil War. His very existence struck me as remarkable.

As I look back at those childhood days of voracious reading I am more and more convinced that it matters very little what a child reads so long as he enjoys it. It is the reading habit which counts. With time and maturing taste and tactful parental suggestions the quality will improve. At least it will for those children who are destined to read with any discrimination. It is better to read poor books than no books. There is always the chance of reading good ones by mistake and enjoying them. Many a non-reader or poor reader has learned to enjoy good books quite late in life.

When I was a boy, for several years my favorite author was Sir H. Rider Haggard, whose romances of adventure in Africa, in lost civilizations and in the historical past excited my imagination more than have any books before or since. An old distinction used to run that a romance is a story centered on action and plot and a novel is a story centered on character. This is probably the essence of the matter, but there is more to romance than that. A romantic novel does not have to concern itself with love or sex (irritating interruptions to a small boy); it does have to intrigue the imagination with the strange and wonderful, with heroic adventure and exotic settings.

These things Haggard's tales do superbly. He was not a writer of the first rank, or even of the second; neither was he a hack. He was richly blessed with the narrative gift, the ability to cast the storyteller's magic spell. He wrote with intimate authority about Zulus and the African wilderness because he had seen them as a young man and had never recovered from the experience. He had a boyish delight in battles, perilous journeys, fabulous cities and magnificent adventures. Encountered at the right time in one's education, Haggard is perfect. He is the quintessence of the romantic. What if his characters are elementary, his prose flat and his plots fantastic? An enthralled child cannot be distracted by such trivial blemishes.

But there is more to Haggard than his romantic appeal. A child is always a hero worshipper. He admires d'Artagnan, or Richard Coeur de Lion or Babe Ruth and unconsciously absorbs ideals based on what he believes, often erroneously, to be the standards of his hero. And in the old hunter Allan Quatermain, hero of more than a dozen of Haggard's best romances, any child can find a hero worthy of his worship. Allan is not subtly drawn, but he is believable and he is admirable. Courageous, a dead-shot and a master of the African wilderness, Allan Quatermain was also a man of honor, a sentimental man irreproachably devoted to the memory of his two wives, a modest hero and a loyal friend.

To be smitten with admiration for Allan Quatermain as I was at the age of twelve is to have a higher ethical ideal than one can hope to emulate. Although Allan was not an aristocratic English gentleman, he abided by the highest concepts of the gentleman's code. Chivalrous without being priggish or unbelievably virtuous, modest, kind and generous, Allen Quatermain is a more practical and effective model of ethical behavior than most boys encounter in life or in Sunday School—at least in Sunday School as I knew it.

Because both my grandfathers were pillars of the First Baptist Church, my parents were raised in nearly identical atmospheres of conventional, nineteenth-century, evangelical Protestant faith. As children they went to church twice on Sundays and to prayer meeting on Wednesdays. They did not object. Everyone they knew did the same. But by the time they were bringing up children of their own, they and a large proportion of the population

of their country felt more relaxed about church attendance. Once on Sundays was enough, and prayer meetings were ignored. They sent their children to Sunday
School, and after Sunday School they waited in church in
the family pew for their children to join them.

Entering church was an ordeal for a child as self-conscious as I was, a child who couldn't buy a five-cent candy
bar without blushing and fearing that he might say the
wrong thing and so incur the storekeeper's scorn. A small
door opened from the Sunday School into the church, not
decently in the rear but right up front a few feet from the
platform on which the minister stood. By the time Sunday
School was over, most of the congregation was seated in
church. One had to walk out in front of everybody, across
the front of the auditorium and up the center aisle, with
hundreds of eyes watching to see if one's hair was brushed,
if one's Eton collar was still safely anchored to its collar
button, if one seemed as embarrassed as one was.

In Sunday School we were introduced to the most popular Bible stories. Religion as worship, as communion with
deity or even as ethics was rarely mentioned. It would have
been awkward, anyway, when we had so many more important things to worry about in Sunday School, such as
which class would get a gold star for the best attendance
record. Our teachers were young, incompetent, easily flus-
tered by disconcerting questions. Although I was shy, I
was the annoying child who always asked them: How could
Noah have got a polar bear for the ark? Where did Cain's
wife come from? Long before I knew what the word skepticism meant I was skeptical. It was my own idea and I don't
think that any book or individual influenced me in this respect.

As long as my grandparents lived my parents went faithfully to church and took their children with them. But after they no longer needed to fear hurting their own parents, their attendance became less and less regular. I don't think that either my mother or father was ever really religious. Religion for them was a matter of social conformity, of respectable behavior and of honorable conduct. As the twentieth century progressed and it was no longer necessary to attend church regularly to be respectable, they drifted away, secure in the knowledge that their personal conduct was as irreproachable as it had been in the years when they were exposed to three doses a week of Baptist doctrine. But by the time I realized that my mother and father were no longer Baptists except in an hereditary sense, I was seventeen or eighteen and had acquired convictions of my own.

When I was a child Cleveland was a large city but not so large that Society with a capital "S" was not still a fairly homogeneous unit. Its members did not all know each other, but they generally knew of each other. They knew where one another's money came from, from steel, or coal, or automobiles, or lake shipping or Standard Oil or whatever. They belonged to the same clubs and only three country clubs counted. They sent their children to one or the other of two private schools for boys and two private schools for girls. They sent them to dancing classes conducted by a lady who boasted that the social contacts of several younger generations were all made under her benign influence. And the women read the society weekly whose editor boasted that she was the arbiter of Society, that those she mentioned belonged and those she did not did not.

A child was not consciously aware of all this. Nothing about it was obtrusive. There were no dominating families with the rigid traditions and hereditary snobbery of the proper Bostonians, or with the sense of caste of the fastidious Philadelphians. Cleveland was too young and Middle Western for that. But Cleveland was old compared with the cities of the farther Middle West. It had none of the rawness and bustling ostentation which many writers have described as typically American and archetypically Middle Western. Perhaps the New England influence was responsible for a certain sedate tone about Cleveland. The city was largely created and its mold set by New Englanders from its beginnings, for it was originally part of Connecticut's Western Reserve.

"Tell me about when you were little." Millions of parents have tried to respond to this often repeated request with small success. They are astonished to find how little they remember. It may all be there, the world of their childhood, as carefully preserved in the subconscious mind as the newspapers in a time capsule, but without the aid of a psychoanalyst's flattering interest, very little of it is readily accessible. I can remember only a few dramatic high spots—the time the Pekingese rushed out of the Corletts' upstairs sitting room and bit me in the left calf, the time the storm came up at Mentor Beach and I saw the blue-gray body of the drowned woman, the time the big boy threw my cap out the trolley car window. But most is lost.

Probably many people remember their childhood in far more specific detail than I can. Nevertheless, the quantities of verbatim conversation set down in many autobiographies arouse my skepticism. It may be only a convention. The author doesn't really claim that he remembers the exact words, but the convention is misleading and hovers on the verge of fiction. Skilled writers of autobiography sometimes recapture the child's point of view with dazzling success, and the illusion of childhood relived which they create inspires me with profound admiration. My memories are too fragmentary for such a feat, even if my skill were great enough.

Well into the present century it was the fashion to regard one's childhood as the happiest time of one's life, and to recall with poignant nostalgia the halcyon days when the hills were so much higher and a bright sheen of wonder lay upon the world. In childhood, it was claimed, life was new and exciting and at the same time wonderfully secure. But with the growth of psychological theories about the sinister importance of infant environment and the parallel growth of self-pitying revelations in autobiographies, childhood is no longer a predominantly happy time in literature. Writers remember hardships and privations, frustrations and psychological trauma, teachers they feared and fathers they hated, nasty talk and brutal bullying.

I am more fortunate. When I remember my childhood in the big brick house with enormous gables on Fairmount Boulevard or at Winden, I find that my memories are neither particularly happy nor unhappy. I lived from day to day, accepting everything in my experience as normal and natural—as do most children. Acceptance, I think, is the key word of childhood. Without standards of comparison, a child accepts everything as the way the world is. It is only as he grows older that he notices the differences.

With the wisdom of hindsight and some knowledge of what the childhood of most human beings consists of, I must conclude that my childhood was almost like a pleasant dream. Certainly it did not include any major fears or alarming crises. I could live quite safely in my imagination most of the time, sharing the wonderful adventures recorded in books while experiencing few indeed of my own. It wasn't until I was sent away to boarding school at fifteen that life suddenly broke in two. Without any preparation whatever I discovered that the world was a difficult and frightening place and that I had no idea how to cope with it.

· *two* ·

Growing up is a curious business. It is never a smooth and orderly progression. We mature in fits and starts, getting ahead in one respect and struggling desperately to catch up in another. In my case the process was painfully uneven. When my mother deposited me at a famous New England preparatory school I seemed old to some of my classmates. And I was old in my distaste for the organized bedlam of boarding school life, in my conspicuous lack of the physical exuberance which drives so many boys to any activity so long as it is noisy and strenuous, and in my bookish knowledge and intellectual interests. So my odd nickname was probably well deserved. I was called "Pater."

But I soon discoverd that I was also much younger than most of my classmates—in my abysmal lack of social self-confidence, in my innocence of the ways of the world and of schoolboys in mass lots, and in my ignorance of many of the practical details of life. I remember that I did not know how to buy a railroad ticket (I thought that Pullman berths came automatically with railroad tickets); did not recognize a bill for what it was when I received one; did not realize that when the mathematics teacher bellowed with rage, growing so red in the face that apoplexy seemed imminent, he was just teaching according to his usual methods and was not consumed with personal scorn and hatred for me. Life for a boy with my ill-digested, bookish sophistication and my social naïveté would have been difficult enough in any preparatory school. At Arnold it was gruesome.

Arnold was not the school's name. I have called it that because when I was there the school was wretchedly run and I do not wish to criticize the present school, which, no doubt, has changed for the better in more than thirty years. Situated among beautiful, rolling New England hills with several small lakes nearby, Arnold made an attractive first impression. When Mother and I arrived we were ushered into the headmaster's office and greeted with icy formality by a large, bald, beady-eyed individual with a luxuriant mustache. He informed us that my application had been received late, that the school was crowded, and that consequently I was not to live in one of the regular dormitories, but would stay at the village inn until things could be straightened out. This did not sound promising, but it turned out to be far worse than it sounded.

During my year at Arnold I lived in seven different lodgings. This meant that a shy and timid boy never got settled anywhere, never lived anywhere long enough to become well acquainted with the boys around him. The worst of it was that my longest single stopover in one place was in the senior dormitory, where I was the only new boy in the building. And at Arnold "new boys" were not spoken to by "old boys." It was one of their "traditions." So for three months I lived like a social pariah or a casteless Hindu. Older boys passed me in the hall, but did not see me. No one so much as looked inside my room and, of course, I never dared look inside anyone else's. It still makes me angry to recall those dreary days.

I realize, now, that my plight was caused by administrative carelessness, indifference and inefficiency. At the time, however, I was filled with furious resentment at what seemed to be deliberate persecutions. The man who symbolized everything I disliked about Arnold was the pompous and arrogant headmaster, who strode through the corridors with his academic gown swirling around him, refusing to speak to any of the younger boys because he had never bothered to learn their names. Nor did I react with visible enthusiasm to Arnold's innumerable traditions.

These struck me as absurd. Most of them were intended to make Arnold resemble an English public school without the actual physical hazing. "New boys" said "Sir" to "old boys"; never passed an "old boy" when walking without politely asking permission, which was not always granted; never walked down a corridor or across a hallway, but always sidled along making sure that the right sleeve of their jackets brushed the walls. Although such traditions were childish and silly, they were not unbearably irksome. They did contribute to the prevailingly foolish and artificial atmosphere of the school.

Even more foolish was the organized effort to generate an entirely synthetic school spirit. All boys were supposed to love Arnold with a feeling too deep for tears. Attendance at all athletic contests was compulsory and any lack of spontaneous enthusiasm in cheering was publicly denounced at school meetings. I still remember with considerable pleasure the school meeting which was the climax to my disillusionment with the Arnold spirit. The president of the senior class—a handsome youth who looked much like my mental picture of Amory Blaine, hero of

Scott Fitzgerald's *This Side of Paradise,* which I had read shortly before coming to school—made an emotional address. He urged us not to succumb to our depression, not to be too discouraged or unhappy, to realize that it was always darkest just before the dawn. Now was the time which would be the crucial test of our Arnold spirit. I can't recall whether he sniffled audibly or brushed an imaginary tear from his eye; but I do remember wondering what on earth he could be talking about. In a moment the cause of his grief and of his inspiring address to the student body was made clear. The hockey team had lost two consecutive games and the basketball team had lost three! My disgust at such cant was only equaled by my self-satisfaction at being superior to it.

My migratory existence at Arnold, my obviously bookish interests, my lack of social ease with other boys and my hearty dislike of the school and all its works combined to isolate me and to throw me back upon my own resources. I was unhappy, but in a restrained way. I just felt scornful of anything Arnold approved (which included algebra and Latin, alas!) and therefore constrained to find a pleasanter and more rewarding life in books.

My English class was assigned *A Tale of Two Cities, Ivanhoe, Silas Marner* and *Julius Caesar,* and I had read them all before. So I bought books in the village, Westerns by Max Brand and Tarzan tales by Edgar Rice Burroughs. And I made the school library my own. Often I had it all to myself. And there I read a wild mixture—Shakespeare, whom I liked, and Ariosto, who bored me dreadfully, and Kipling. I already knew the Jungle Books and *Just So Stories.* But it was at Arnold that I discovered the fascinatingly worldly Mrs. Hawksbee in *Plain Tales from the Hills, Soldiers Three* and privates Mulvaney, Ortheris and

Learoyd, *The Man Who Would Be King, Without Benefit of Clergy* and *The Finest Story in the World*—and a
score of other masterpieces by the greatest master of the
short story in English literature. My excitement and delight were intense, and I had no one with whom to share
them. Here was a writer telling as romantic tales as Rider
Haggard's; but I was three years older than I had been at
the peak of my Haggard enthusiasm and I could see that
Kipling was an immeasurably greater writer.

At that time, the winter of 1921-1922, no one had yet
denounced Kipling for his politics, his ardent faith in the
British Empire. If anyone had, of course, I wouldn't have
known it. The important thing to me was the incredible
magic of Kipling's virtuoso verbal skill, his authoritative
manner, the rich color and exact detail of his pictures of
Indian life, or of life on the Roman Wall, or of life anywhere else. I was dazzled and enthralled, and read right
through Kipling's complete works until I came to his
history of the Irish Guards in the First World War, which
brought me to a full stop.

Kipling was the first writer who made me see beyond the
pleasure of the story to the writer telling it, who made me
notice not only what he said but how he said it, who made
me aware that there is something strange and wonderful
called literary craftsmanship. Kipling was particularly
useful for this, because in his inferior stories his tricks and
mannerisms are clumsy and intrusive. I first realized while
reading Kipling that a man can be a very great writer and
still write badly part of the time, or even a good deal of
the time.

Kipling also contributed to my education in a non-
literary sense. It was he who first introduced me to the fact
that a woman no better than she should be can be intelli-

gent and likable as well as dangerously charming, that brave and honorable men are behaving quite naturally when they are attracted by such women, that moral questions can be infinitely complicated and difficult, with no blacks and whites and with uncountable shades of gray. Life, evidently, was filled with problems which were not discussed in Sunday School and which had not been emphasized in the romantic fiction I had been reading with such avidity.

Although Kipling, particularly in his younger days, liked to pose as a worldly and sophisticated writer, he was fundamentally a moral one. The imperialism he championed was an ideal, not just a system of conquest and exploitation. It may have been a narrow ideal based upon an arrogant theory of Anglo-Saxon superiority. Nevertheless, it was a noble ideal, for it stressed absolute obedience to the code of an officer and gentleman, responsibility for the welfare of others, hard work, courage, gallantry and loyalty. Kipling was not a doubter. He believed in human beings and in their ability to live up to their obligations and their duty to do so. Although a few of his stories are sentimental and a few are unpleasantly brutal, most are not.

Only the futilitarians of our unhappy age of disillusion and despair would claim that it is sentimental to abide by codes of honor, to serve a cause which seems good and to die for it if need be. Millions of people have died for the cause of freedom since Kipling wrote, but without the unquestioning conviction of Kipling and his characters in the value of their sacrifice. That they lacked such a conviction is one of the saddest aspects of our modern world. Kipling was not a thoughtful writer with a carefully considered philosophy of life; but his flaming faith in honor and courage and loyalty is an essential part of any man's equipment for living. Without such a faith life is too dreary and mean for any more profoundly thought-out philosophy to be of much significance or use. Consequently, I believe that any fifteen-year-old boy who falls under Kipling's magic spell is lucky.

Looking back after so many years to my year in Arnold's ivied halls it seems incredible to me now that I could have behaved as foolishly as I did. Because I was lonely and depressed, resentful of the school and scornful of the more childish antics of my fellow pupils, I withdrew into myself. Fearful of rebuffs, easily dismayed by the loud laugh that spoke the vacant mind, I ceased trying to make friends. This was natural, I suppose, under my special circumstances. But natural or not, it was a mistake. It merely postponed for a while the essential lesson of learning how to get along with strangers in a world I never made.

Even more foolish, incomprehensibly so to me today, was my refusal to admit the necessity of applying myself to subjects I disliked. I knew, of course, that they had to be passed before I could enter college. But I avoided thinking about such a harsh reality and made no serious effort. I studied as little as possible, did poorly in everything except English and continued to read as many books as possible, often in times which would have been better spent studying algebra and Latin.

To make everything more difficult I was sick frequently (psychosomatic illnesses?). I succumbed to influenza twice and was in and out of the infirmary regularly with a plague of boils and a mysterious skin infection. Autumn and compulsory football gave way to winter and compulsory gym work, followed by spring and compulsory baseball. I was moved, for the last time, into a dormitory inhabited solely by boys of my own class. Lilacs bloomed and the seniors made impassioned speeches at school meetings about their last term on the dear old hill. This, they said, was the summit of their youth, a sacred interval charged with painful emotions. Would the new boys please be even more inconspicuous than usual in order not to mar their remaining days by needless reminders of their uncouth presence? Before I realized it the year was over, and Mother said I did not have to go back. I had never told her how much I disliked Arnold, but it was obvious that my year there had not been a success. But that left a pretty problem on her hands. What to do with me next year?

· three ·

Mother's solution to the educational problem of her youngest son was drastic. She probably reasoned that since my year at a large school had been a dismal failure, a small school would be the answer. She chose what must have been the smallest school in the United States. The Bridger Ranch School was situated near the head of a high valley in the middle of the Rocky Mountains. In no proper sense of the word was it a school at all. Actually, it was a scheme dreamed up by the proprietor of one of the oldest dude ranches in the business to insure that some income could be counted on all the year round and not just in the three months when Eastern guests paid to "rough it" in luxury on a Western ranch.

How Mother heard of Bridger Ranch I do not know. But I remember well the eloquence of the ranch business agent who came to see us at Winden. He spoke of the finest teaching methods and small classes, of personal instruction, of tennis courts and a swimming pool—all in the glory of snow-capped peaks, with daily horseback riding and frequent camping trips into the mountains. How could any mother searching for a school for her difficult son resist such an appeal? How could any boy who had read much about the West resist it? Bridger Ranch sounded perfect. How imaginative that agent was I discovered on the first day I arrived.

When my father and I walked into the train shed of the Northern Pacific Railroad in Chicago that September of 1922, we knew that the headmaster of the Bridger Ranch School would be waiting in the Pullman car in which all the boys from Chicago and points east had reservations. Standing on the platform near our car was a man who looked less like a schoolteacher than do most bartenders and race-track touts. He was tall, lean and bald. His nose was craggy and he wore a trim military mustache. He glared out at the world with a tough, belligerent stare. A two-thirds smoked cigarette hung precariously from his lower lip. "Are you for Bridger Ranch?" he asked.

My father blinked with surprise. "Yes," he replied. "I'm O. W. Prescott and this is my son."

"Pleased to meet you," said the rangy man. "I'm Colonel Bolt, U.S. Marines retired. I'm sure your son and I'll get along fine. I'm used to handling men and I don't expect I'll have any trouble handling boys. What're you going west for, son? Girl trouble, one girl or too many girls?" His beaming leer was meant to be friendly, but its genial lewdness appalled me and I blushed in a frenzy of embarrassment.

The Colonel introduced us to another teacher. Mr. Harrigan was short, plump, with a snub nose and childishly innocent blue eyes. Before further conversation could take place the conductor shouted; I said good-bye to my father and the train began to roll.

Within a few minutes I learned several important facts the ranch business agent had somehow forgotten to mention. I discovered that the Bridger Ranch School did not yet exist. It would come into being with our arrival and that of several boys from Texas and the Pacific Coast. I discovered that neither the Colonel nor Harrigan had been a teacher long. I learned that the student body would consist of a grand total of eighteen boys. And almost as promptly I realized that close association with the Colonel and Harrigan was going to be an eye-opening experience for a boy whose life had hitherto been sheltered.

Trains were not streamlined and Diesel-powered in 1922. It took us three days and two nights to reach the town of Carson. But the trip was exciting. As a student of the works of Zane Grey I found it exciting to see the corn fields and pastures of the Middle West give way to the bunch grass of the high prairie, and at last to watch the dim, blue line of the Rockies slowly rise above the western horizon. And it was exciting, and alarming, too, to listen to the Colonel and Harrigan. They talked interminably, getting acquainted with each other, showing off before their youthful charges.

The Colonel's past was colorful. He had fought at Belleau Wood and in the Argonne. He had been stationed in Peking and had a wife and numerous children in Honolulu. Why he had left the Marines was not quite clear, something involving liquor and women, he hinted. To meet a man who had been involved with liquor and women and to have him for my school headmaster seemed to me altogether extraordinary.

Harrigan had also fought in the First World War, but he was not a professional soldier. After the Armistice he had remained in Paris, doing what I don't remember if I ever knew. But to hear him and the Colonel exchange reminiscences about their amatory adventures for the amusement of a dozen open-mouthed schoolboys was indeed a revelation, one kind of amateur progressive education. We weren't "learning by doing"; but we certainly were learning from those who had. And all this before the train stopped briefly at Carson, a dingy little town surrounded by sand, sagebrush and high mountains.

In Carson the proprietor of the Bridger Ranch awaited us. Randolf Saunders was without doubt the handsomest man I have ever known. Tall, straight, with classically regular features, flashing blue eyes and a beautifully waxed mustache, Randy looked exactly like the Charles Dana Gibson illustrations of the hero of Richard Harding Davis' *Soldiers of Fortune*. He was dressed in a resplendent version of what the well-dressed rancher should wear: a large Stetson, a coat of soft tanned elk hide, a red scarf at his throat and glittering cowboy boots. He informed us that a prolonged rainstorm had made the dirt road to the ranch impassable. We would have to wait in Carson for a few days.

After three days the road was still too muddy for cars, but Randy was impatient. He hired an old-fashioned stagecoach, which had seen service in one of the national parks, and assembled a group of horses. We started out, eighteen boys arrayed in newly purchased cowboy finery, Randy, the Colonel, Harrigan and the stagecoach driver. We took turns riding in the coach and on horseback. The horses' hoofs made sucking gulps in the mud. The coach horses soon tired. We boys, unaccustomed to long hours in the saddle or cramped in the old coach, soon tired, too. The fifty-five-mile trip took two days. We spent the intervening night in the bunk house of a friendly rancher.

Bridger Ranch lay at the head of a high valley. A river fed by melting snow flowed down the center of the valley and high mountains towered on either side. Several were capped with snow. Cottonwood trees grew by the river and pines on the lower slopes of the mountains, which were bare rock above the timber line. The air was sweet with the smell of sagebrush and everything was so beautiful that I didn't notice for an hour or so that there was no swimming pool and there were no tennis courts. They were planned for some indefinite future, and the ranch business agent had lied as brazenly about them as he had about the finest teaching methods. I didn't care a bit. Who would want to play tennis or go swimming when he could live in a log cabin and ride horseback surrounded by such beauty?

We lived two boys to a log cabin. The food was good. The scenery was wonderful. Daily horseback riding was fun. And the Colonel and Harrigan were not exacting teachers. The Colonel would sit on the back of his neck with his feet propped several feet higher than his head on one of the logs in the wall of his cabin and ask questions out of a Latin or an algebra textbook. He had passed both subjects creditably sometime in his youth, but he made no pretense of expert knowledge. Harrigan, who taught English, history and French, was not much more authoritative; but he tried a little harder. Both men were more interested in enjoying life in the West, and that, of course, was what we boys were most interested in.

Although Colonel Bolt had served on three continents, he had never been in mountain country before. But lack of confidence was not one of the Colonel's shortcomings. He knew all about everything and had done everything. After lunch one bright afternoon in late September a week after we arrived at Bridger Ranch, the Colonel strutted out in front of the rest of us and called for silence. Right then he was going to climb the mountain ridge immediately west of the ranch. Who wanted to come?

Harrigan, with the wisdom of an old soldier, said that his feet hurt and retired to his cabin with the newest issue of *Adventure Magazine*. A dozen boys volunteered. But, as the Colonel and any Zane Grey reader should have known, distances are deceiving in the bright, clear air and high altitudes of the Rockies. We set out about two o'clock, one impulsive, swaggering ex-Marine and twelve green, adolescent boys. At five o'clock the sun had disappeared behind the western ranges and steel-blue shadows were racing down the slopes. We were tired, hot, thirsty, and only about halfway up the ridge. The ascent had not been difficult by Alpine-climbing standards, but it had been for us. The Colonel was breathing as heavily and was as drenched in sweat as any of us.

How he hated to admit that he had misjudged the height of that mountain ridge! But it was getting darker fast. We should have turned back long ago. Reluctantly and somewhat shamefacedly the Colonel ordered us to start down. Shivering as the evening grew colder and the last sunlight left even the mountain peaks on the eastern side of the valley, we scrambled along trying to retrace our tracks. "It looks like we'll be a little late for supper," said the Colonel. "Come on now, boys, double quick march!"

We hurried as best we could. But the mountain side was steep, covered wtih huge boulders and tangled with a scrubby growth of jack pine. It was already so dark that we were in considerable danger of tripping and breaking an ankle. Suddenly we heard a familiar sound, the ranch dinner bell ringing far beneath us. And then we could see the faint and distant gleam of the carbon lamps shining through the dining hall windows. "Last lap," said the

Colonel, and then without warning he yelled so shrilly that we all jumped as if a banshee had shrieked in our ears. Colonel Bolt had nearly fallen over a one-hundred foot cliff which stretched away as far as we could see on both sides. That, certainly, wasn't the way we had come up!

With great difficulty we slithered to a stop beside the Colonel. The ledge on which he was standing was about ten feet wide and sloped at an angle of about thirty degrees. On one side was the cliff, on the other the slope we had been descending, which was so steep we had been joking about the impossibility of climbing up it. And on that slanting ledge we spent the night. In the darkness we did not dare try to find a way around the cliff for fear of falling off it. "Rim-rocked," said our youngest member, a boy from Carson who tried to impress the rest of us with his familiarity with Western lingo. "Nothing for it but to sleep," said the Colonel. "It'll be a good experience for you. Toughen you up. But for God's sake don't lie sideways to that cliff and roll over. Feet down, heads up, everybody!"

Sleep was impossible. Nights are cold at eight thousand feet in the Rocky Mountains in late September. We had set out in shirt sleeves without sweaters or jackets. We were hungry and could hear the dinner bell which some thoughtful soul kept ringing to guide us home. We were thirsty and could hear the tinkle of a nearby stream which we could not find in the dark. We were acutely uncomfortable on that gravelly slope. And we were afraid that we might doze and roll over the edge in our sleep. Naturally, no one slept. I remember thinking to myself, You wanted adventure in the West, well, this is it, you might as well enjoy it. And oddly enough I did, not the cold and discomfort, but the thought of what a wonderful letter home I would write if I ever got down from that cursed rim-rock.

Next morning as soon as it was light we saw cowboys from the ranch start up the mesa trail leading many rider-less horses. It was obvious that they were going to bring the horses as near us as possible. Then they would work side-ways on foot across the face of the ridge until they could rescue us. Colonel Bolt was embarrassed and angry enough already without this additional ignominy. He was damned if he was going to be rescued. "Come on, boys," he growled. "Got to get out of here before those boy scouts push us back in wheel chairs."

Now that the sun was up we could see how lucky we were. The cliff was several hundred yards long and the shelf on which we had spent the night was only about forty yards long. If we hadn't hit it just right on our climbing, sliding, sitting descent in the dark, we would have had no place to stop when we reached the cliff. And if it had not been for the recklessness of our fatigue and ignorance, we wouldn't have dared come down that slope at all. When several boys tried to climb up it they could not. But some thirty feet above us the slope ceased being a semi-cliff and slanted back at a safer angle. If we could only get that far before the rescue party reached us, we could insist that we had not needed to be rescued. Finally the boy from Carson, who was lithe and agile, managed the climb, taking with him a length of clothesline which the Colonel had brought with him.

But Paul wasn't strong enough to hold anyone else on the rope and there was no tree or stone to which he could tie it. All he could do was dangle the rope so the next boy could hold it for moral encouragement and to help his balance. And as more boys held the rope from above, more weight could be put upon it from below. When my turn came I was about ten feet up the bank before Paul's heels dislodged a stone. It struck me on the top of my head and knocked me backwards onto that narrow, sloping shelf. Luckily, the Colonel (the last to leave the sinking ship) kept me from rolling off. I was dazed, but still managed to make the climb. And so did everyone else, just in time, too, just before the cowboys arrived with ropes and sandwiches and led us back to the waiting horses. We were back at the ranch at two o'clock in the afternoon, exactly twenty-four hours after our departure.

Although I had had a few riding lessons in an indoor ring in Cleveland, my riding skill was negligible and my extensive knowledge of horses was as theoretical as my other animal lore. So the daily riding which was the chief excuse for being at Bridger Ranch proved more strenuous and exciting than I had expected. Two striking personalities were responsible for this—Colonel Bolt, who insisted on teaching us equitation and polo, and Marjorie, who regarded me with such intense suspicion when we first met that I recoiled in some alarm, never suspecting how great our mutual love would become.

Marjorie had a china-blue, frenziedly rolling wall eye, a sway back and a spine like a ridge pole, spavins, white spots on a buckskin hide and a pessimistic disposition. She was a scrawny Indian-bred pinto who had never been thoroughly broken and who had just spent two years on the open range. Too fatalistic and gloomy to be a dangerous bucker, she was too hysterical and independent to be cooperative. Her name had been Spot. I renamed her in honor of an Alabama accent that had recently enchanted me, but whose owner's full name I can no longer remember.

Marjorie had forgotten anything she had ever known

about bridles, reins and saddles. I knew precious little about them.. We learned together. It was hair-raising for a while—for a long while—because I believed in kindness to animals, and the cowboys and other schoolboys didn't. They believed in force, which always gets quicker if less satisfactory results. I was kind to Marjorie, but Marjorie was not often kind to me, at least at first. Bridling Marjorie taxed all my eloquence. Saddling her sorely tried my patience. Mounting her required good luck as well as good management and all the courage I could muster.

Marjorie would stand the length of my arm and the length of her reins away from me and defy me to come closer. After I had crawled up the reins and flung them over her neck she would spin like a dervish and back up like a switch engine. As soon as I dared touch the stirrup she would plunge into her jolting gallop. Once I was aboard, Marjorie would insist that she had no idea what reins and bit were for and she never let her right foot know what her left was doing. Long before we reached a compromise settlement of our differences the Colonel's ideas brought new hazards into our lives.

His equitation class meant jumping hurdles and doing tricks in a ring, bareback. Because of Marjorie's peculiar figure, with that spine of hers rising up like a picket fence, I suffered acute discomfort and never had a flat surface on which to stand or jump or lie according to the Colonel's commands. I longed to swap Marjorie for another horse, any other horse, at least during equitation. But loyalty forbade and I could not hurt her feelings. We were beginning to care. For months I had shamelessly bribed her with oats. Now that our destinies were linked I could not forsake her.

Polo was less painful because we used saddles, but even

more surprising to Marjorie. She would never turn around without discussing the issue and sometimes not even then. So there were certain difficulties. Once we were lucky. The ball was in the right place and we were in the clear. We took it the length of the field at a full gallop to the cheers of our side. But, unfortunately, Marjorie, although a slow starter, was at last worked up into the spirit of things. She wouldn't stop galloping. She left the polo field blithely behind her and carried me a mile down the road. We left in near triumph and returned in disgrace.

Finally, the oats, or my considerate treatment, or perhaps a heart of gold beneath her unprepossessing exterior, prevailed. We publicly displayed our affection. Marjorie would come when I called her and follow me like a dog, a unique spectacle in that still moderately tough mountain country. It fascinated cowboys for miles around. But our happiness was short-lived. Marjorie caught her hind feet in the corral fence, fell backward, rupturing various internal organs, and died with her head in my lap. Cynically amused onlookers took photographs of our last parting, for which I have not forgiven them yet.

There were dogs at Bridger Ranch, too. Although it was often twenty or more degrees below zero in the winter, the official ranch policy was to leave them outdoors all night. Naturally, as an animal lover I could not put up with such cruelty. I invited the dogs into my log cabin without worrying about the fact that after the window had been open for a few minutes they were little better off. The wolfhound would lie on the side of my cot with his back wedged against the log wall and his legs stretched over the hollow where I slept. The collie would lie at the foot with his legs tangled among the wolfhound's. Then I would crawl in. And then the two Scotch terriers would jump on top of the three of us, making five in all. It was a trifle crowded and they squirmed and kicked until morning, but I slept the sleep of the just. I knew that no one else at Bridger Ranch was so kind to animals.

It wasn't only horses and dogs that made life exciting to a young animal lover. The ranch was only a few miles from a national park, and wild animals sometimes forget to pay attention to official boundaries. On our short rides in the valley and in the foothills we were constantly meeting game, and on our pack trips into the mountains we saw more. Deer were always about, eating the horses' hay, trampling the cabbage patch nightly until Randy lost his patience and scared them off by firing his shotgun. Coyotes howled in the horse pasture only two hundred yards from our cabins. Elk roamed the lower slopes of the mountains, and mountain sheep often grazed on a bluff which projected from the mountain ridge.

I remember the heart-in-the-mouth excitement I felt when I first saw a buck and several does soar away with the wonderful springy bounce of deer in a hurry; the majestic spectacle of a bull elk outlined against the sky as he stood on the crest of a small foothill and impatiently tossed his antlers; the alarming size of a bear's tracks in the snow and my disappointment that I never saw a bear. But the animals were only picturesque and beautiful. It was the people who made life at Bridger Ranch an educational experience. And chief of these was Colonel Bolt.

It was the Colonel, I am certain, who first jolted me out of my private world of boyish dreams and vicarious bookish experience into a sudden awareness that here right before my eyes was a fantastic human specimen, and that it was time to sit up and take notice of the people around me. The Colonel, I now know with the wisdom of many years'

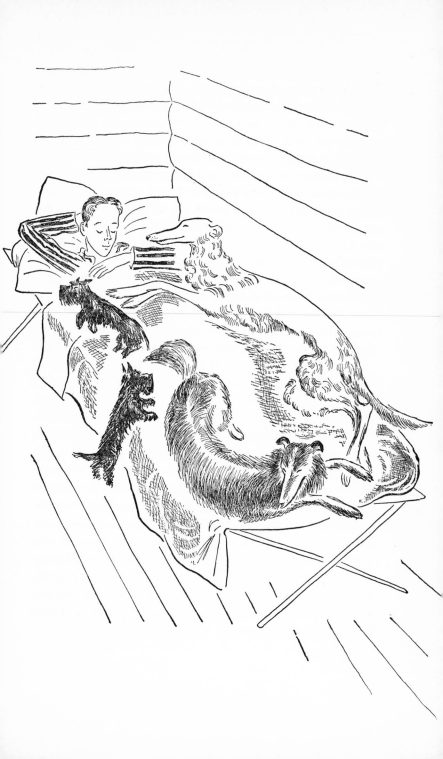

hindsight, was not so extraordinary as I then thought him. It was my inexperience and the oddity of such a man being the headmaster of a boys' school which made him seem so. Still, school headmasters don't customarily swear like cavalry troopers, delight in telling dirty stories, and frequently fortify themselves with mountain dew.

On Saturdays the Colonel would sometimes hop the mail truck into Carson and not come back until Monday. He made friends up and down the valley and cultivated a social life of which we boys knew little. The first time I saw the Colonel celebrate his defiance of the Volstead Act was a cold night in early December. Some six inches of snow covered the valley floor. About one in the morning I was awakened by yells of rage and a chorus of booming guffaws. The noise came from the next cabin but one. Almost immediately the same commotion broke out in the cabin next to mine. While I was still sleepily wondering what was up, the Colonel and Harrigan burst into my cabin. "Hold him," shouted the Colonel. Harrigan did. And then the Colonel thrust two heaping handfuls of cold snow down my pajama neck and proceeded to massage my chest and stomach. My roommate received the same treatment, and further offstage cries were proof that no one was being overlooked.

Such antics didn't seem funny at the time. The Arnold headmaster would certainly not have indulged in practical jokes. The Colonel's breath had been distinctly noticeable. Could he have been drinking? I knew from his conversation that he considered whiskey one of the blessings of civilization. But would he indulge so conspicuously right under Randy's nose? Would he risk his job by a performance which would certainly set all eighteen boys talking. Would he!

Several weeks later we went to a dance in the one-room schoolhouse twelve miles down the road toward Carson. Some of us rode through the wintry night on horseback and some got a ride on a truck. The schoolteacher was the only unmarried girl at the dance and the Colonel monopolized her. Ranchers, ranch hands and cowboys leaned against the wall in morose silence. A violin and accordion supplied music, and an old man with an Adam's apple like a tennis ball called the square dances. None of us had seen a square dance before, but we danced anyway—with leather-faced women whose husbands had ridden bucking broncos in Buffalo Bill's show, with young wives who kept watchful eyes on their husbands' frequent trips to the stable where jugs were kept with the horses, and with the several women whose husbands were Eastern remittance men.

Suddenly a burst of scornful laughter called attention to the Colonel. Standing in the middle of the schoolhouse floor, he was boasting that he could kick a cigarette from the lips of a man several inches taller than he was. He did, too, but he split his pants in the process, thus insuring the success of the party. Riding home in the truck, the Colonel was obviously exhilarated, even to eyes with little experience in judging such matters. He sang gaily and shouted that high kicking was the least of his accomplishments. "Whee! Whee! See that snowdrift," cried the Colonel. "Whee! I'm Douglas Fairbanks." Spreading his arms in a perfect swan dive, he dived from the tailboard of the truck, hitting the snowdrift precisely in its center. Unfortunately, the drift wasn't as deep as the Colonel's exuberance had led him to expect. He landed with a sickening thud and knocked himself unconscious.

Most of the boys at Bridger Ranch were refugees from the rigors of orthodox higher education. Some had been ill and had fallen behind. Several were stupid and lazy, and several were "problem" boys. With life so full of exciting new experiences it did not occur to any of us to worry about the shortcomings of our curriculum or about the Colonel's and Harrigan's casual performance as teachers. Boys have a sublime gift for taking things for granted. They may marvel at a teacher's personality, but they are unlikely to question his qualifications to teach at all.

So when late in April I discovered that neither Colonel Bolt nor Harrigan had ever heard of the College Entrance Board examination system, I was not unduly alarmed. Neither, needless to say, were they. Only one other boy was planning to take the examinations, anyway. The Colonel shrugged and offered out of the kindness of his heart to drive us to Denver in June when examination time came, Denver being the nearest city where the examinations were given. He didn't have a car, but he would have one by then, a Buick on which he expected to make the first payment by June first. Denver was only some 700 miles away. Several of the highest mountain passes in America lay between us and Denver. The roads were dirt all the way. But we would get there easily in a day and a half.

We did, too, but not easily. We started at four in the morning and drove without stopping except for gasoline and hamburgers until three the next morning, when we collapsed into bed in a hotel in Cheyenne. The Colonel drove every mile himself, evidently not trusting Harrigan's driving skill any more than he did Jim's or mine. The Buick was an open touring car, 1923 model. The Colonel drove it the way he rode a horse, with reckless skill and grim determination to get all possible speed out of it. We made 500 miles that first day, which is a long day's drive even on modern paved roads. On the dirt roads of those days it was prostrating. But bright and early the next morning after less than five hours' sleep we were rolling on to Denver and a batch of College Entrance Board examinations, which I took with the innocent optimism of trusting youth. After all, I had had no trouble passing everything satisfactorily at the Bridger Ranch School. Needless to say, I failed the five examinations I took. My year at the ranch had been highly educational, but not exactly in the academic sense.

What Randy thought of the singular headmaster he had employed he kept to himself. In fact, if he thought at all he kept it to himself. A more taciturn man never lived in that mountain country where men were traditionally strong and silent. The only clues to Randy's character were his taste for finery in Western costume and his pride in the handsome palomino horse he rode. Randy was an Easterner, a Harvard graduate, the successful operator of a large dude ranch. His speech, when he spoke at all, was cultured and correct. His manners were ceremonious. And he was married to a blonde from Carson with a voice like a rusty saw and the mind of a cheerful schoolgirl. Sometimes when Olga shrilled forth some particularly fatuous remark, I thought I saw Randy flinch, but I was never certain.

Although it was the Colonel who jolted me into fascinated observation of the adults around me, there were plenty of other people in the valley who repaid study. I soon decided that Randy was too aloof for me to approach and that I knew all there was to know about Olga after the second time I played hearts with her, a game she found difficult and endlessly fascinating. There was the Swede, a cowboy and trapper of such prodigious strength that he was reputed to be able to make a horse scream by the pressure of his legs. I myself saw him squeeze the open ends of a horseshoe with one hand until they met. There was the forest ranger, a little man who wore a revolver just like cowboys in fiction and the movies. Once, when he was properly primed with a few drinks, I saw him shoot at a tin plate thrown in the air and hit it four times out of six.

And there was the Governor, an old man who had never been governor of anything, but who had led a life of far-wandering adventure. "My mother," said the Governor to me once, cocking a bloodshot eye, "made me promise never to take the name of my God in vain. And I never have. But she didn't say anything about killing men and I've killed a few, quite a few." Since there was no way of telling how much of the Governor's talk was true, I chose to believe everything he said. It was more fun that way.

Several of the neighboring ranches were owned by Easterners who preferred the life of the West, or who settled there because their families preferred to be separated from them by several thousand miles. Some of them ran a few head of cattle, or raised a few horses, or boarded a few dudes during the summer; some just lived the informal, outdoor, pleasantly alcoholic life which a small but regular income made possible. We became acquainted with several of these "ranchers" in a casual fashion and I learned to know two of the women "ranchers" quite well.

Both were charming, well-educated Eastern women. Both were married to men who could not share their cultural interests. Both at that time were in their middle thirties and both were gracious and kind to a sixteen-year-old schoolboy who was conspicuously grateful for a chance to talk about books. Otherwise they were unlike.

Elizabeth Olmstead was tall, slim, with a luxuriant mass of bright golden hair and an expression of habitual sad tension. I thought her beautiful. She lived on a small ranch about five miles away on the other side of the river. There was one other boy in the school who shared my passion for books. He and I used to ride over to call on Elizabeth frequently—that is, we used to until her husband objected.

Why Jack Olmstead objected was a mystery. Greg was a willowy youth who could never have made any husband in his right mind jealous. I was shy, innocent, idealistic and romantic. To me Elizabeth was culture and beauty in the wilderness. She was the kind older woman who introduced me to the delights of reading Edna St. Vincent Millay and James Branch Cabell, who lent both of us books and played to us on the piano. Lonely and apparently unhappy, she was probably flattered by our admiration. She never so much as flickered a flirtatious eyelid at either of us. Nevertheless, Jack Olmstead forbade her to receive us any more and our visits ceased.

Of course, we were thrilled by such a dramatic development. We believed that Elizabeth was unhappy. Now we were convinced that she was a romantic and tragic figure persecuted by a jealous oaf. She was a member of a family of wealth and social prominence, a Boston one, I think, but it might have been Philadelphia. In her early twenties she had visited a dude ranch where Jack Olmstead was employed as a cowboy. He was handsome when I knew him. He must have been considerably more so when he was younger, before he stopped shaving regularly. Elizabeth eloped with him to the horror and consternation of her family.

Whether her marriage was as unhappy as Greg and I thought it must be, whether it endured after I left the valley, I do not know. My memory of Elizabeth is more untrustworthy than most of my Western memories, not only because of the distortions of time, but also because Greg and I may have misunderstood the circumstances and been misinformed about them. Nevertheless, I have never forgotten Elizabeth Olmstead and I shall always be grateful to her. She looked stunning on horseback in her divided leather skirt. She read poetry beautifully. She was thoughtful and kind. She stimulated my imagination immensely. Years later I wrote a short story about her, a crudely melodramatic one I fear, which I submitted to a number of magazines. It was rejected by them all, a blessing I failed to appreciate at the time.

A mile nearer, but also on the far side of the river, was the Miller ranch. Biff Miller enjoyed sufficient income so that he could operate his small dude ranch with careless unconcern. A profit would be fine; but it was more important to ride a good horse, to play polo and to spend much time enjoying good drink and good company. Such habits didn't endear him to his wife, who divorced him a few years later. But when I knew Judith Miller she was still putting up with Biff, cursing him in a semi-humorous fashion, striding about in manure-stained blue jeans, feeding animals, cleaning stables, cooking, doing every kind of chore for which her upbringing should have unfitted her.

Judith Miller was a short, trim, chatty woman with black eyes and a cigarette perpetually in her mouth. At that time, of course, few women smoked and precious few wore trousers. Judith fascinated me. She came from Baltimore, from an old family which included several well-known soldiers and one distinguished ambassador. Obviously she was a lady; just as obviously she didn't choose to act like one. What Judith really liked were books, music, the theatre, art, and good conversation lubricated by a few drinks. Such tastes, plus her casual manners and her indifference to her appearance, ideally qualified Judith for Greenwich Village. Instead she lived in lonely exile in the middle of the Rocky Mountains.

Like Elizabeth Olmstead, Judith seemed to enjoy talking to Greg and me. She told us about her literary and artistic friends, about the new plays she had seen on her last visit to New York two years before, about Edgar Lee Masters' *Spoon River* and Eugene O'Neill's *The Emperor Jones.* She lent me volumes of Victor Hugo.

Because of their similar interests I expected Elizabeth and Judith to be friends. They lived only a few miles from each other and were the only two people in the valley who habitually read books. But as far as I could see, they didn't care for each other. And in this, too, I may have been wrong. A schoolboy, excited by my discovery of the rich variety of human personality, flattered by bookish conversation on an adult level, I was probably too busy absorbing new impressions to see much below the surface. I enjoyed talking with both women, and that was enough. They supplied an element of civilized culture in an environment which, though picturesque and intellectually stimulating in its own way, had few ties to the world of books.

But even at Bridger Ranch I managed to make literary discoveries. In a forlorn collection of abandoned books left behind by summer guests, I found two extraordinary historical novels by Edward Lucas White, a minor American novelist who deserves to be better known than he is. They were *El Supremo,* a massive and fascinating study of the great nineteenth-century dictator of Paraguay, Francia, and *Andivius Hedulio,* a novel of picaresque adventure in the reign of Commodus which provides a superb panorama of the Roman Empire.

And I stumbled quite by chance on a little green-bound volume called *Kokoro*, by a writer with the strangely musical name of Lafcadio Hearn. I had never heard of him. But for several days, while the Chinook wind blew down from the Tetons and the coyotes howled not very far outside my window, I snatched every moment I could to read stories and legends about old Japan told in what then seemed to me the loveliest prose I had ever read. The enthusiasm I felt did not flag for several years, not until I tracked down a good many other Hearn books. But eventually it subsided and became only a dim memory. Many years later when, as a literary critic, I had occasion to reread much of Hearn the experience was disillusioning. He had not worn well, and since he had not changed, it was plain that I had. And I became convinced that Lafcadio Hearn, like numerous other writers, is best read by the young. The hot-house aroma of his overly mannered style is best appreciated at an age when the blissful intoxication of words leaves no critical hangover.

Because the Colonel and Harrigan demanded so little of their pupils, I had plenty of time to read. Besides the literary driftwood I picked up around the ranch, I read books I brought with me, books borrowed from the tiny Carnegie Library in Carson, and those Elizabeth and Judith recommended. I even read pulp-paper adventure magazines, which, I have since learned, have been the favorite reading matter at Western ranches since the first longhorns were driven north over the old Chisholm Trail. And then sometime in the spring an idea smote me like a revelation.

Why should I waste time reading anything which wasn't really good, anything which did not add to my knowledge of the great world of books, for me the most important of all worlds? And I swore a mighty oath by all my private gods to read nothing thereafter which was without recognized literary merit. For a year or two I kept that resolution absolutely, and for many years I kept it more or less, with only an occasional backsliding when I could not resist sampling some currently popular best seller such as *Beau Geste* or *The Sheik*.

One sunny Sunday in May when we were all at dinner in the mess hall, someone shouted, "Fire!" Everyone rushed outdoors and there sure enough was a thick column of smoke rising from the cottonwood grove where our cabins were located. What fun! What delicious excitement! But it didn't seem quite so delightful when we reached the fire and I discovered whose cabin was burning. It was mine. A small crowd of ranch hands, schoolboys, Randy, Olga, the Colonel and Harrigan surrounded the burning cabin. Flames were consuming the roof, but so far the walls were untouched. Someone had carried out a pile of my clothes. Someone else was throwing a bucket of water from a safe distance. But what about my precious books?

Without any process of conscious thought, without any decision that now was the time for an heroic gesture, just conforming to any book lover's normal instinct, I dashed into the burning cabin. A shout of warning and surprise rose from my astounded friends. But it changed to laughter and ironic applause when I emerged with an armful of scorched books. I still have some of them, their spines cracked and blackened by the heat but their print still readable: a copy of *Roget's Thesaurus*, which I have never found very useful; Donn Byrne's *Messer Marco Polo;* James Branch Cabell's *The High Place*. They are dear to me, proof that a dedicated book lover, when his passions are aroused, can be a man of swift and appropriate action.

Two other aspects of life at Bridger Ranch were more matters of imagination than of fact. The first was my constant wonder and joy at being in a Rocky Mountain valley at all. Smelling sage, hearing the mournful lament of coyotes, and finding odor and sound both exactly as my imagination had pictured them were exciting pleasures. Memories of scores of books, many of them excessively bad books, kept me company every time we rode a narrow trail through a canyon or over a mountain pass, every time I listened to young cowboys joking or to old timers yarning about the good old days.

I knew the constant joy of finding expectations fulfilled, of seeing, if not particular historical sites, the kind of country in which Kit Carson and Jim Bridger had trapped beaver and fought Indians. "This is the place," said Brigham Young, indicating the spot where Salt Lake City would be built. This is it, I felt, the West I have read about, looking much as it always had even though my scalp was in no danger—as the Governor claimed his had been when he first entered the valley. Only a schoolboy with a romantic imagination could have taken such intense pleasure in merely being alive in such a place. I had that kind of imagination then.

The second aspect of life at Bridger Ranch which meant much to me was scenic beauty. A young child does not notice scenery or derive any aesthetic pleasure from it. The ability to do so usually comes in adolescence. To some it never comes at all. I have never learned to take as much pleasure in flowers or in a beautifully decorated room as many women and a few men do. But the beauty of landscape excites me, and it first did so at Bridger Ranch. The

mountains rose sharply on each side of the valley and at its head was an extinct volcano with snow in its crater the year round. I can't forget the jagged silhouette of the horizon; or the gray-green of the sage, the rich brown of the mountain cliffs, the suddenness with which white clouds sailed into view from their hiding places in other valleys and other states, the pastel shades of sunsets reflected on snow, and the blue and bottomless depths of the sky at evening. All one had to do was to look up and there was beauty, inconspicuous in the folds of the foothills, majestic on the mountain heights, pure and lovely in the clear air of those high altitudes. I looked up constantly.

· *four* ·

Although my first year at Bridger Ranch was a complete failure scholastically speaking, I had obviously enjoyed it and benefited by it. So my parents allowed the eloquence of that ranch business agent to persuade them to send me back for another year. I think that his clinching argument was that the Colonel would not be present and that an Episcopal minister would be taking his place. Randy was not one to make the same mistake twice.

There were a few more boys the second year and four teachers instead of two. The teachers were competent and reasonably exacting. The minister (such a contrast to the Colonel!) was a high-minded, well-intentioned individual without a trace of a sense of humor and with no gift for getting along with adolescent boys. He did his best, preaching solemnly every Sunday morning, reproving our language, which needed it; fighting conscientiously with his temper, which he usually controlled, but always with painful difficulty. A dull and unhappy man, the nicest things about him were his pretty wife and his gurgling baby daughter.

That second year at Bridger Ranch was considerably more sedate and consequently less stimulating than the first. The novelty of the West had lessened. And the Colonel with all his magnificent vitality, his cheerful vulgarity and his unpredictable enthusiasm for folly was not there. I missed him. I had not respected him, but I liked him.

Once I met him on the streets of Carson, unshaven, bleary-eyed, obviously at a dead end. We shook hands formally and I had the tact not to inquire about the Buick. The first payment was the only one he ever made. During the ensuing year bits of gossip about the Colonel dribbled in. Then they ceased. I hoped and still hope that he rejoined the Marines or went to Mexico as he used to dream of doing, or that he found some "last frontier" where he could be happy.

At the conclusion of my second year at the ranch, my mother and sister joined me for a tour of the West, which included Yellowstone, Salt Lake City, San Francisco, Yosemite, Los Angeles and the Grand Canyon. Although I passed most of my College Board examinations that June, back home at Winden we were still confronted by the problem of my education. I had lost one year when I was demoted a grade on my arrival at Arnold and another by the fiasco of my first year at Bridger Ranch. Soon I would be eighteen, and college was far away. The time had come for drastic measures. A tutoring school seemed to be the solution, one of those institutions of the 1920's which specialized in teaching boys precisely what they needed to know to pass examinations—with no concern for general education.

Plymouth Academy was transformed into a conventional preparatory school many years ago. But while I was there the headmaster who brought about that change was making his first tentative gestures in that direction. The school was one of the oldest in New England and had known many changes of character. As a tutoring school it was one of the best in the business, which meant that its students resembled the boy refugees I had known at Bridger Ranch except that there were many more of them. Some were lazy, some stupid, some dreamers who had not "learned how to study." Some were rebels in full revolt against education and others wobbled on the edge of juvenile delinquency.

These were the wastrel sons of sudden wealth, tough, raucous and obnoxious. Several years older and several sizes larger than most schoolboys, they made the football team a terror to other schools and life difficult for the Plymouth teachers. On Saturday nights they got drunk and on their return early Sunday mornings they bellowed lustily in the halls. Their ideas of humor were primitive, and on at least one occasion included leaving contraceptives on the school lawn where they were sure to be seen the next morning. And they could not be expelled. At least, they weren't and I concluded that they could not be. The school needed their tuition and the athletic teams needed their brawn.

The remarkable thing about Plymouth was that most of its students passed the College Entrance Board examinations and entered the country's leading colleges. There was no nonsense about the teaching. These are the things you have to know in order to pass, declared the teachers. This is the way the examiners' minds work. These are the questions asked for the last six years. This year's won't be the same, but they will be similar. Remember, remember, remember!

It wasn't intellectually stimulating, but it was effective. We did remember and we passed. I didn't pass everything my first year at Plymouth, but the fault was mine. I still found mathematics so dull and difficult that I flinched from the necessary effort and read books instead. The second year I passed everything, with plenty of time left over for more books.

Just as the Colonel and life in the West were educational, so were the Plymouth roughnecks and life at the school. Today I think that my five years spent in odd educational circumstances helped me greatly in my progress toward some degree of intellectual and emotional maturity. But I believe that they also did much to strengthen my instinctive emotional reserve. I had always been shy, envying but not understanding the gift of easy fellowship. Except for Greg at Bridger Ranch, I found no friends who shared my consuming interest in books. Many boys could not understand such an obsession. Some scorned it. Naturally, I drew into myself. I acquired a self-sufficiency which enabled me to get along with composure and even with contentment without close friends—and which, of course, made it more difficult to make them. I learned not to care a hoot what the roughnecks thought and I learned to avoid their crude ridicule by keeping my own thoughts largely to myself.

Of course, no boy in his teens ever learns to be a Lord Chesterfield of glacial poise and suave social hypocrisy. I never pretended emotions I did not feel. I never expressed opinions I did not hold. But I began to appreciate the value of thought before speech and mastered my first lessons in silence. It would have been a good thing for me in later life if I had remembered those lessons more often than I did. I was destined to make some frightful mistakes by not keeping my mouth shut and I still don't keep quiet as much as I should. But at Plymouth I grasped the basic idea and established minimum diplomatic relations with numerous young barbarians I privately considered obnoxious.

Recalling the comparatively solitary life I led at Plymouth, it is somewhat surprising to me now that so many of my Plymouth memories are pleasant ones. One of the pleasantest is my brief career as an athlete. It was during my second year when the school took on a new sport, fencing. I had never fenced, but I had read so many historical romances that I had a vivid mental picture of exactly how it ought to be done and of myself doing it.

Dumas had not been very explicit about d'Artagnan's technique. But Rafael Sabatini in *Scaramouche* had written a wonderful scene in which his hero lay in bed and developed a philosophy of dueling. Sabatini's hero thought of an attacking lunge, of his opponent's parry, of his next thrust, and of his opponent's logical next counter. And instead of stopping there, he carried his train of thought through three or four more exchanges.

I tried to do the same. In the excitement of a match I could not often do it. My opponents usually behaved quite contrary to my expectations. But by imagining that an inter-school fencing match was a duel with one of Cardinal Richelieu's crack swordsmen, I kindled in myself a wonderfully uncharacteristic *élan*. There are three kinds of swords used in fencing. I used the epée, the nearest in shape and in the rules of its use to a seventeenth-century rapier. I lacked the strength to handle a sabre and the finesse for a foil. But with my imaginary dueling sword I was surprisingly successful.

For the first and last time in my life I made a varsity team. I won the majority of my matches. And to my intense delight I won the New England Interscholastic Championship in the epée. To crown my moment of glory, when the Plymouth team participated in a tournament with some members of the United States Olympic team I won one match. It was probably pure luck, the expert not taking a schoolboy seriously. But the thrill was sweet, and the major "P" I was awarded in a minor sport gave me an enormous satisfaction.

At Plymouth there were few rules. Many Saturdays I took the interurban streetcar and called upon several Cleveland girls, including my sister, at a nearby preparatory school for girls. On many other Saturdays I went in to the nearest city, sometimes in a group, sometimes alone, to see a movie or a play. And I experimented with more rarefied varieties of art, a recital by Paderewski and a dance performance by Ted Shawn and Ruth St. Denis. I found an excellent book shop and patronized it regularly.

At Plymouth I edited the school magazine, wrote both verse and prose for it and did my best to drum up interest among potential contributors. And I found two English teachers who were glad to talk to me about books.

Both were able men who fretted with exasperation because of the necessity to teach Burke's speech on *Conciliation* year after year to meet the demands of the College Entrance Board examination system. One was a devout Roman Catholic who had written an epic poem about the crucifixion of Jesus which had been published in a Catholic magazine. The other was a likable and witty young man who yearned to be a sophisticated writer in Greenwich Village, but who, unfortunately, had to earn his living teaching an odd lot of boys in a tutoring school. In return for reading and commenting on my poems and stories, he used to make me listen while he read out loud from the letters he wrote to his friends. These were composed in a style more elaborate than anything written since the death of Walter Pater.

But the Plymouth teacher I remember best was Mr. Barnes. For forty years before he came to Plymouth he had taught Latin at one of America's most celebrated schools. Perhaps his radical political ideas had made it necessary for him to change his job so late in life; or perhaps he had just passed the retirement age and needed to keep on working. In any case, Mr. Barnes was a striking figure with a deeply lined face and a thatch of thick white hair more like a world-famous poet's than an obscure teacher's. A few days after I began his course in Virgil I arrived early in his classroom and found him alone. He looked at me sharply. "Boy," he said, "I've noticed you always have books under your arms which aren't texts. You like to read, do you?"

"Yes, sir," I said. "I'm reading Galsworthy's . . ."

"Ever read *Progress and Poverty?*"

"No, sir."

"Ever heard of Henry George?"

"No, sir."

"Greatest book since the Bible. Greatest man since Lincoln. If you want an education and don't just want to pass a few silly examinations like everybody else around here, you ought to start by reading that book."

Although I never did read *Progress and Poverty,* from that day on I made a point of arriving fifteen minutes early at my Virgil class. Mr. Barnes was always there. In answer to my persistent questioning he told me all about the virtues of the Single Tax, which, I suppose, was as good an introduction to economics as many another. Mr. Barnes did not persuade me that the Single Tax was a good idea;

he did convince me that economics was a more important and more dramatic subject than I had supposed and that he himself was a fascinating individual. Although his knowledge of Latin literature was immense, he had been teaching elementary Latin too long and had lost interest. His class was dull. But whenever he talked about politics, economics or history, his face became animated, his eyes flashed, and a torrent of facts, figures and prejudices would overwhelm his hearers. He was the first radical reformer and social crank I ever knew.

While I was at Plymouth I read three British authors who ignited explosions in my mind like a chain of intellectual firecrackers. They were Thomas Hardy, George Moore and Oscar Wilde. All three forced me to think about ideas and issues which had been simmering on the back of my mental stove for some time. In their simplest terms the germinal ideas were Hardy's morose and angry fatalism, Moore's aesthetic hedonism and Wilde's cynical amorality. Confronted with such challenging attitudes toward life, I felt compelled to think them out as best I could, to decide what they meant to me and what I myself believed about these weighty subjects.

It was *Tess of the d'Urbervilles* which was my introduction to Hardy. I can't remember whether I noticed Hardy's crudities of fictional craftsmanship at that time. I was overwhelmed by his bleak philosophy. Here was a great writer and a shrewd observer of life who wrote with pity and indignation about human beings who were helpless victims of blind chance, a chance which Hardy seemed to regard as positively malignant. Although I knew theoretically that misery and suffering were inherent in the lot of man, I had had no personal experience of them. I had already concluded that the conventional doctrines of Protestant Christianity did not seem reasonable to me. But could I share this furious gloom? Could I accept this complete negation of the existence of a benevolent deity?

I wasn't sure. On my next trip to the city I bought *The Return of the Native* and *Jude the Obscure*. I read and pondered them. And, being young, healthy and without personal griefs, I could not find the world as dark as Hardy did. Of course, I could not foresee how dark the world would be within a few years for many millions of people. But just brooding with Hardy completed my rejection of orthodox religious dogmas. I found that I was a natural unbeliever, and recognition of the fact brought no shock or painful disillusion.

The unbelief I reached in my teens still persists. It is not a matter of aggressive certainty, or of scorn for the beliefs of others. The positive convictions of atheists and of old-fashioned scientific materialists seem to me to be ignorant, stupid and vulgar. The universe is so full of inexplicable mysteries that negative certainties seem to me as foolish and arrogant as doctrinaire convictions. I have no idea what the answers may be to all the great questions which men have asked for some six thousand years. And it is beyond dispute that a great many men more learned than I have believed joyfully and triumphantly in matters which seem to me wonderfully unlikely.

That puny reason is incapable of judging eternal mysteries is a standard rebuttal to doubts like mine, and a pertinent one. But, it seems to me, such reason as we possess is all we have to judge with. Many people rest their belief on their faith in the authority of others who claim divine inspiration. I respect their conviction and recognize the comfort it must be. But I am incapable of sharing it. The prophets and mystics who claim special knowledge of God's will and that they have enjoyed communion with Him do not persuade me. There are so many of them, all communing with different gods and reporting different versions of ultimate truth. Since most of them must be suffering from illusions, I find it impossible to admit that any particular one of them is more right than the rest.

The ethical teachings of the great religions seem to me sublime and beautiful, much the greatest achievement of mankind. The only long-range hope for the world lies in the possibility that men and women may some day act upon them more than they do today, with more love for their fellows. It is the claims of supernatural authority advanced by all religions which I have never been able to accept. That one religion is truer than another, or that one religious leader is more truly inspired, or that one improbable dogma is true and another is false—such concepts seem to me unworthy of serious consideration. But I know that many noble minds I deeply respect do take them seriously. So I am left quoting Santayana, who is generally too cold-blooded and detached from struggling mankind for my taste, but who expressed more perfectly than anyone else I know of what seems to me the only truth about religion which an unbeliever can believe: "Religion is valid poetry infused into common life. It is not a revelation truer than perception or than science."

That religion is one of the most interesting, significant and universal manifestations of the human spirit, all history shows. Religious feeling has inspired many of the noblest and most beautiful achievements of men, and religious doctrines have inspired the finest ideals conceived of by men—the sacredness of the individual, the brotherhood of mankind, the golden rule. But these noble ideals are valid in themselves and do not depend upon belief in the more peculiar ideas of St. Paul, St. Augustine, John Calvin or John Wesley. And the peculiar ideas of these and other religious leaders have divided men into clashing cults and drenched the world in blood. I am convinced that the beautiful truths of religion are those on which men of all religions and denominations, or of none, can agree.

Some people argue that without belief in divine control of human affairs and in divinely apportioned rewards and punishments after death, there can be no ethical standards and no reason why we should not treat each other like starving wolves fighting over a carcass. This argument makes little sense to me. Many firm believers have acted abominably and have justified their crimes because of their beliefs, Torquemada, for instance. Many unbelievers have been humane, honorable and idealistic. Human beings are influenced far more often by what they believe to be justifiable conduct than by what they believe to be the ultimate justification. A decent man acts decently, whether he is a Christian, Moslem, pagan or philosophic skeptic. A wicked man or an irrational fanatic acts abominably no matter what his theoretical religious convictions.

If we believe that honorable conduct is imperative because of our self-respect as human beings, that cruelty to others is the unforgivable sin because it destroys persecutor and persecuted, then we will not torture and massacre and deliberately corrupt. Such belief in the basic decencies must be taught by parents to their children, by teachers to their pupils, by writers to their readers. If they fail to do so, civilization will collapse and religion alone will be powerless to prevent it. For the sad truth about all religions is that only a few of the faithful make any serious effort to abide by the higher teachings of the religion which they nominally profess. Most men accept religious ideas and then pigeonhole them for further reference in some indefinite future. Or they deliberately choose which ideas and teachings they will believe, selecting those which are not troublesome, which do not conflict with a competitive, materialistic way of life; yet they still think of themselves as religious when they are nothing of the kind. They don't realize that to be a good Christian, for instance, is not the same thing as being a good provider, a good citizen and a decent chap. It is immensely difficult to be a good Christian, so difficut that only a very few men in 2,000 years have achieved it. In fact, it is so difficult that most men don't even believe it is desirable.

Most men in every century since the crucifixion have believed in only some of the teachings of Christ. Nominally Christian, they do not believe in non-resistance to evil, in selling all they have and giving to the poor, that the meek shall inherit the earth. On the contrary, they believe in fighting evil with a punch in the nose or with a thermonuclear bomb, in as much wealth as they can obtain, and in aggressive enterprise. An unbeliever who shares these beliefs is not troubled by pangs of conscience. He does not try to delude himself that the goals and standards almost universal in Western civilization are Christian. For him it is difficult enough to try to live up to a code of honorable conduct, and he feels certain that loving kindness and generosity are high enough ideals for fallible mortals. The extremes of abnegation and self-sacrifice have always been beyond the capacity and alien to the aspirations of all save a few saints.

I know that such ideas may seem crass and materialistic

to many people. But I know also that in matters of faith and doctrine people believe what is natural for them to believe, not what it might be nice to believe or what others think that they should believe. If we think seriously at all, we believe what we must believe. There is no choice. Some people are destined from birth by the very nature of their genes and their glands and their blood stream to be believers, others to be unbelievers. Some people are born to conform to traditional ideas, or to fashionable ones. Others are born skeptical.

Nevertheless, I do believe that there is one absolute obligation in belief which applies to every man and woman of good will: if we hope that men will act in any way superior to the behavior of beasts, we must believe in moral restraints and ethical obligations, in duty and honor, in kindness, in mercy and in love. Whenever the majority of men cease to believe in these basic ideals, free civilizations are doomed and we might as well surrender to the first dictator who promises us the moon in a basket if we will connive at his abominations.

In the last few pages I have skipped past more than thirty years, from the impact of Thomas Hardy on an eighteen-year-old schoolboy to some of the convictions I now hold. A similar chronological mix-up is unavoidable in describing the results of my discoveries of George Moore and Oscar Wilde. The Moore I discovered was the author of *Confessions of a Young Man* and *Memoirs of My Dead Life*—not the author of that memorable example of literary naturalism, *Esther Waters,* nor the consummate stylist who wrote *Héloïse and Abélard.* That early Moore was an insufferable poseur, a fatuous young snob intent on shocking his Victorian readers into moral convulsions, a man infatuated with the vilest purple rhetoric and in love with his own image as an aesthete and as a joyous pagan lover of the perverse.

Like Dickens' famous fat boy, the young Moore wanted to make his readers' flesh creep. He did mine, deliciously. What a revelation his books were! Here was a famous writer who not only denied the orthodoxies of religion, but who scoffed at conventional morality. Moore seemed to acknowledge no values except aesthetic ones and seemed to recognize no goals except pleasure, the more fleshly the pleasure the better. He insisted that the cruelty and suffering which built the pyramids were entirely justified by the pleasure the pyramids offer to the contemplation of a cultivated élite. He boasted of his dissipations and gloated over perverse follies which were probably imaginary. And he argued that aesthetic beauty has no connection with morality, which is true; but he also insisted that immorality is in itself beautiful, which is false.

Reading Moore I was forced to think about morality and inevitably turned first to the question of sexual morality. Although the idea is always in the air, it was Moore who first persuaded me that a love affair unsanctioned by church or state wasn't necessarily immoral; that it could be natural and delightful. But it was plain that to George Moore a love affair was the supreme expression of love between the sexes. And that was silly. Obviously, love enriched by the partnership, loyalty, compromise and shared experience of a successful marriage would be infinitely more rewarding than a mere love affair. I only sensed this vaguely then. But I know it now.

Although George Moore's early works were adolescently perverse, they were filled with ideas new to me. Moore's glorification of aestheticism, of art as the supreme human achievement and of art for art's sake, was stimulating.

It was obviously not the whole truth of a philosophy to live by, or even of a philosophy of art. But there was an important half truth in his argument—the significance of a work of art in itself as a creation independent of social and moral factors.

Shortly after I discovered Moore, I encountered Oscar Wilde. Naturally, since the way was prepared, there was no great shock. But Moore took himself quite seriously and was neither witty nor gaily cynical like Wilde, who could sum up a similar aesthetic hedonism in a neat epigram. "There is no such thing as a moral or an immoral book. Books are well written, or badly written. That is all."

This was a bolder statement when Wilde first wrote it, and even when I first read it, than it seems today. It isn't true; but it is partly true. The subject matter of a book can neither be moral nor immoral. A novel about saints is not necessarily moral, and one about depraved sinners is not necessarily immoral. The skill of writing is everything to the artistic success or failure of a novel; but it is an artistic factor, not a moral one.

The moral or immoral element is intention. A book intended to persuade its readers that cruelty and incest are virtues instead of evils would be profoundly immoral. But a book which seeks to explore the psychological origins of cruelty or incest would be neither moral nor immoral. And moral questions in literature are not always clarified even when intention seems plain, because our judgments of intention may be faulty, warped by our preconceived beliefs based upon particular customs, traditions and religious doctrines. Nevertheless, somewhere in our thinking about morality we are forced to fall back on axiomatic truths. If you do not believe that it is axiomatic that cruelty is evil and kindness good, if you insist that "everything is relative," then you deny that moral questions exist or are worth consideration.

At eighteen, however, one doesn't stop to evaluate every glittering epigram tossed off by an Oscar Wilde. One just rejoices in their wit and refuses to take them seriously. "Conscience and cowardice are really the same thing." One smiles and may not realize until many years later how profoundly immoral such a flippant epigram is. For Wilde's intention was to make the action forbidden by conscience seem courageous. He didn't mean that walking on the grass would be courageous if one's conscience forbade it. He meant to justify his own unhappy and self-destructive life.

My youthful consideration of metaphysics and ethics, although earnest enough, was neither prolonged nor profound. I have no illusions that my present reflections on the same subjects are sensationally significant. I have neither a religious bent nor a philosophical mind. But I do believe that certain issues cannot, or rather should not, be avoided. How dull it must be not to know what one thinks! The unexamined mind like the unexamined life is a closed door barring one of the most interesting rooms in the experience of being human. It is true, of course, that the majority of people do live without troubling to decide what they think, and some of them are as happy as pigs in clover. But surely many of them would find life more interesting if they thought about it.

It may be too obvious for comment, but if I should have any young readers, perhaps I ought to remind them that my first serious struggle to think about ethics occurred when Calvin Coolidge was in the White House. That was the jazz age, the age of the sheik, the flapper and of flaming

youth, of Prohibition and the bathtub gin, of post-war disillusion and of Freud, of H. L. Mencken, Eugene O'Neill
and Sinclair Lewis, of automobiles parked on dark roads
as well as in motion.

It was fun and exciting to be young then. New ideas
made the very air seem invigorating. New freedoms were
noisily proclaimed. Among them was the freedom of respectable girls to drink bootleg liquor and not forfeit their
claim to respectability, and of nice girls to "pet" or even to
have affairs and still be considered nice. At eighteen I
hardly had enough waking hours in which to absorb so
many stimulating ideas.

In the 1920's elaborate début balls were the fashion in
Cleveland. The girls I took to them or out on dates had
been my friends since childhood and were, as far as I knew,
as virtuous as any Victorian chaperone could have wished.
But I knew others, not my good friends, who were experi-
menting with sex (it was news worthy of gossip when girls
so experimented, not news when boys did) and I heard
much really sensational gossip about the behavior of
young people who were not among my good acquaintances.
Quite a few boys and girls from Cleveland's "best families" were beginning the careers in alcoholism and promis-
cuity which they have pursued ever since.

So perhaps because I am instinctively a planner and or-
ganizer of my own affairs, usually immune to sudden im-
pulses; perhaps because of the hereditary influence of my
long line of New England Puritan ancestors; perhaps because education, reading and the excitement of being
young in a period of dramatic social change were absorbing so much of my time and attention, I postponed my
initiation into the biological aspects of life and cautiously
observed many of the excesses of the twenties from a dis-

creet distance. It would be silly, I thought, for anyone as young and diffident as I to let anything so embarrassing as sex break up his pleasant friendships with girls.

I would not have hesitated to enjoy the delights of a romantic liaison with a seductive siren on the Riviera, but at the moment that was not a practical possibility. And anyway, the problem was not immediately pressing. I had to get into college. In summer vacations I had to play a great deal of golf. And the year round I had to read as many books as possible, particularly books about the Italian Renaissance.

· *five* ·

It was on a still, bright afternoon in the summer of 1925 that I wandered by chance into the unknown country of the Italian Renaissance. I had been reading George Meredith, borrowing successive volumes from the Big House library at Winden, and I walked up through the gardens to return *The Amazing Marriage*. After the delights of *The Egoist* and *Harry Richmond,* that disappointing novel discouraged me and I was ready to forego Meredith for a while. The library was always still. There were only two windows. They overlooked the south and west lawns and were enormous, but somehow there was never enough daylight in the library. What light there was, reflected from the green lawns outside and shining on the green rug inside, seemed almost as if it were green, too. The book shelves filled all four walls and soared as high as I could reach. Those on the east wall were protected by locked doors of handsome bronze grill-work and housed Grandfather Sherwin's rarest books. Over the fireplace in the north wall was a large marble mantelpiece. Carved on this was an heraldic shield with Grandfather's Latin motto: *"Video, Audeo, Taceo."*

After putting *The Amazing Marriage* back in its proper place, I browsed idly along the shelves. Two-thirds of the shelf space was occupied by my grandfather's angling collection, but there was plenty of space left for sets of the standard classics and for volumes of biography and history. In the history section my eye fell upon a small volume bound in blue, something about an Italian city of which I had never heard. Why I pulled it out I do not know, but I did and it fell open at page 47 and I began to read:

"Now the man of whom I told you, the servant from the house of the Baglioni who ran to see the truth of that which the watch at the gate had told, came and found the enemy at San Luca, and he escaped away and ran and came to the house of his masters and found his Highness Semonetto Baglioni, son of Ridolfo, and spake and said to him, 'Go not forth, my Lord, for the enemy are all in the town and have nearly reached the Plazza.' To this he answered and said, 'Rather will I die in this fierce strife than let my enemy drive me out of my house to beg my bread.' And when he had said this, alone as he was, having with him no companion, with his shirt on his back and his stockings on his feet, with a buckler on his arm and a sword in his hand, he went forth against the enemy; and under the archway of the Court House of their Highnesses the Priori he met the enemy who was just then coming into the Plazza. Forthwith he set upon the foe and did battle with him bareheaded as I have told you and in his shirt; and no man born of woman was ever seen of so high a temper and so brave, and full sure am I that never again in Perugia will be seen a man of such dreadful daring.

"He was at the present eighteen or nineteen years old, he had not as yet shaved his beard, yet so strong he was and so courageous, so fitted for deeds of arms that he was the world's wonder; and he tilted so gracefully and bravely as to pass the belief of every man on earth. From morning till night he could have aimed at the bottom of a goblet with his spearpoint and never missed. Peerless was he in all ways, though indeed every man of that house was more worshipful than the other, and they had not equals for deeds of arms."

Could anyone with a romantic imagination resist such enticements? This was not myth or fiction, but the narrative of a contemporary who had seen young Semonetto with his own eyes. Perhaps he had seen that particular battle when the youngest of the ferocious and magnificent Baglioni had rushed forth without armor to attack a small army single-handed. I turned back to the beginning and read for the rest of the afternoon, while the shadows lengthened across the lawns and the tinkle of tea cups sounded from the verandah at four-thirty. The book was *Chronicles of the City of Perugia 1492–1503*, by Francesco Matarazzo, translated by Edward Strachan Morgan.

At that time I had read little history, only school texts in ancient, medieval and American history, and Wells' *Outline of History*. But I had read numerous historical novels, *The Cloister and the Hearth, Henry Esmond, Notre Dame de Paris,* the best of Sabatini and many others. They appealed to the same enthusiasm for romantic adventure which had rejoiced at an earlier age in the stories of Rider Haggard.

And it was this same youthful emotion which was aroused by Matarazzo. His quaint style was charming. His unbounded devotion to the Baglioni family and his reverent admiration for their crimes as well as for their feats of arms were appealing and amusing. The tremendous story he had to tell of battle, murder, treachery and lordly arrogance is one of the great stories of Italian history.

The Baglioni family could boast a dozen members as brave as Sir Launcelot. But, typical Renaissance despots that they were, they were as ruthless and treacherous as Cesare Borgia himself, or, for that matter, as the Visconti, Sforza, Maletesta or Este. It was the gorgeous melodrama of their story which enthralled me. I found it so heady a potion that I read everything else on the Italian Renaissance which the Winden library contained. I bought other books and borrowed still more. The interest in the historical past thus awakened soon widened to include the sixteenth century and, after a few more years, all history.

Such a happy, headlong plunge into history seems to me most fortunate. Too many young people confuse history with dates and with difficult technicalities of constitutional law and economic organization. These are important elements of history and interesting, too, once you have acquired a taste for them. But the taste must be acquired by deliberate and conscientious effort. No effort is necessary to feel the fascination of the more surprising and colorful details of history, such as that the Baglioni were the handsomest men in Italy and kept lions in their palace courtyard, that Anne Boleyn had a sixth finger, that in his old age Henry VIII was so fat he had to be hoisted upstairs by a derrick, that Madame de Montespan was implicated in a noisome poisoning scandal. Such information is history, too, and interesting at first glance.

It is fascinating because human personality and the drama of individual lives are the most interesting things in the world. To see history in such terms is not to see it whole. The view is likely to be obscured by too many

duels, love affairs and narrow escapes. But to read history for its romance and drama is a good beginning. An interest in a colorful individual easily leads to an interest in the problems which confronted him, to the ideas and customs which helped to shape his mind, and to the whole life of which he was a part. One can begin with young Semonetto Baglioni fighting bareheaded in his shirt and soon become entranced by the gaudy panorama of the power politics of Renaissance Italy; and move on from there to the art, literature and philosophy of the period. After one historical epoch comes to life in the imagination, the next step to the majestic spectacle of all history is easily taken. And then it is easy to succumb to the lure of the quest for a philosophy of history, the as yet inconclusive efforts of such scholars as Arnold Toynbee to find some sort of predictable pattern in human affairs.

The pleasures of history are many and various. Even when badly written, its facts themselves are often sufficiently interesting so that they outweigh literary deficiencies. While, contrariwise, if fiction is badly written it is in all save a few notable exceptions beyond redemption. Some of the most famous historical works are, of course, superbly well written, those by Gibbon, Macaulay, Prescott, Parkman and their peers. Unfortunately, precious little contemporary history is written that well. For comparable literary distinction we must turn to historical biographies, to such modern masterpieces as Lord David Cecil's *Melbourne*.

Fortunately, historical biographies provide one of the best and most attractive approaches to historical knowledge. In biography the focus of attention is on one individual, and if he played a major role in the affairs of his time, the author must explain them and in the process supply generous helpings of historical information. Thus, in historical biography the reader gets a balanced ration, personality plus background.

Most history is a record and an interpretation of the past as seen through the distorting lens of an individual mind. The historian must choose much of his data from partial and partisan sources. His selections reflect his personality, his preconceived ideas and his prejudices. The great facts of history are indisputable. Rome fell. But the causes of great events are often unknown or so complex a tangle of many contributing factors that they are subject to violent differences of opinion. Why Rome fell is a matter not yet settled.

But if we cannot be certain of the "whys" of history we can at least inform ourselves about the results, what actually did take place, what kind of men living what kind of lives believing what kind of ideas took part in the Battle of Hastings, or brought about the Industrial Revolution. And finding out such information can be a fascinating, a dramatic and an intellectually exciting experience. History has never been just "past politics." It includes everything human, all mankind's achievements, all its perennial suffering and all its nobility and folly. How could such a study fail to stimulate the mind?

Some knowledge of history is not only an intellectual pleasure, it is also an absolute essential for a sane life in a period of world crisis. One of the most depressing charges against modern education is that little history is taught and that of that little only a trace sinks in. Many supposedly educated people know so little about the past that they are incompetent to think about the present. Most of what they know about the Civil War they learned from Margaret Mitchell and most of what they know about the

American Revolution from Kenneth Roberts—which is better than nothing, undoubtedly, but only a little better. Such people are inclined to confuse Queen Victoria with Helen Hayes and to remember only three citizens of ancient Rome, Julius Caesar, Nero and a fellow oddly called Quo Vadis.

The sad thing about all this is that not only do such people vote; they often also sit in the House and Senate, run big businesses, teach little children and lecture on topical affairs. But to think reasonably about the fearful issues of our tormented world it is essential to know something about the Peloponnesian War, the Punic Wars, the fall of Rome, the rise of national states, the wars of religion, the growth of colonial empires, the rise of capitalism, and the English, American, French and Russian Revolutions. It is also necessary to be able to distinguish between the ideas of Jesus, Dante, Machiavelli, Rousseau, Jefferson, Napoleon, Marx, Lenin and Gandhi. Equally essential is some information about the customary behavior of armed coalitions, about the inflammable ideas about which men have fought in the past, about the nature of men in large masses, and about the nature of the few men who customarily wield political and military power.

Such information does not encourage a facile optimism. The study of history is sobering and does not inspire much confidence. It is certainly depressing to learn about the rulers men have suffered to direct their destinies in the past, for most of them were a sorry lot. But when we consider the incompetency, greed, corruption and stupidity of past governments, we can find some grounds to be encouraged. With all their shortcomings, the non-totalitarian governments of the present are immeasurably superior to their predecessors. Compared with the average run of politicians and statesmen of any earlier century, ours are wonderfully honest and diligent. The exceptional man of genius may no oftener be at the helm of state today; but the witless fool and the scheming knave are less often in power than formerly.

A useful minimum of historical information will not qualify anyone to set himself up as a seer and to prophesy what the Russians will do next week. But it will save him from some egregious errors. It will save him from thinking that problems necessarily have solutions. All too often in history problems were not solved, they were only replaced by new ones. It will save him from thinking that right will necessarily prevail (whose right?), that peace is desired more than power by most political and military leaders, that great changes in the political organization of the world can be made quickly without violence and much bloodshed. An historical perspective does not lead to excessive good cheer. Maybe that's one of the reasons many people prefer to do without it.

Although mankind has not made as much progress as fuzzy-minded optimists believe, it has made much more than the despairing pessimists insist. Cruelty, slavery and terror still walk at large in the world. But more people are leading better lives than ever before, and more people believe that cruelty, slavery and terror are abominable—and this in spite of the pernicious doctrines and monstrous crimes of Russia, Germany, China and Japan.

The basic problem of us all is survival. The nations which value individual freedom must contrive to survive until some unforeseeable shift in the political weather lessens the menace of the totalitarians. This might be a matter of centuries. It could be a matter of a decade. No man can tell. But all men with an adequate knowledge of history do know that political salvation is no easier to find than religious salvation, that it is only reasonable to expect little wisdom from men and from nations (although courage in the face of death can generally be relied upon), and that progress toward a world of peace and brotherhood must be made slowly and with infinite patience. After all, up to the present most men have heartily agreed with Cain that they are not their brothers' keepers.

· six ·

It never occurred to me to go to any college except Williams. My two brothers and three of my cousins had gone there before me. My father and mother assumed that I would go there, too. The possibility that I might wish to go somewhere else was not even considered. One of the reasons I did not consider it myself, I suppose, was that many of the Plymouth boys I disliked were going to Yale, Harvard and Princeton. A college where I would not have to see them again had its attractions.

No one else from Plymouth went to Williams that September, 1926. I knew nobody in the undergraduate body, an experience which was becoming monotonous. I hadn't known anyone when I first arrived at Arnold, Bridger Ranch or Plymouth.

Even an unobservant person who has motored north to Vermont on Route 7 knows that Williamstown and the mountains which surround it in the extreme northwest corner of Massachusetts are beautiful. Tall elms form nearly complete arches over many of the streets. Several of the college buildings are architectural gems and some, which most emphatically are not, have an old-fashioned sort of charm. The mountains did not seem much more than hills to a former student of the Bridger Ranch School, but they could not be more artistically arranged. All day long with every shift of light and cloud they seem to change their color.

Williams did not present the difficulties of adjustment which I had experienced at all three of the preparatory schools. In the first place, I was twenty and most of my fellow freshmen were eighteen. In the second, those schools had taught me much. I had not learned how to be a hail-fellow-well-met or a campus popularity-contest winner. But I had acquired a minimum degree of social self-confidence and I had learned how to conform as much as was absolutely necessary without surrendering any part of my determination to go my own independent way. For four years I led an existence which most students would have found lonely, but which suited me.

I made several intimate friends with whom I played golf, drank bootleg beer, discussed college life, and Life with a capital "L". But these friendships grew out of propinquity rather than because of shared interests. I did not even know many of my classmates well enough to speak to them. But I was by no means a social outcast and I pursued my literary interests without becoming belligerently intellectual. In my junior and senior years, when I had an automobile, I enjoyed motoring over the Mohawk or Berkshire trail to Northampton to call upon girls at Smith College and I also enjoyed convivial evenings in Patsy Ryan's speakeasy in nearby Hoosick Falls. But I enjoyed the Williams library more.

In the 1920's Williams was bound much more tightly in the straitjacket of the fraternity system than it is today. Two-thirds of the students were members. To be one of the rejected third was an humiliation and a public shame, a cruel experience which left deep scars on many a Williams student long past the years of his adolescent tribulations. Freshmen were invited to join a fraternity, or to join a dozen if they were fortunate, shortly after the opening of college, but only after a frenzied week of interviewing and being interviewed, of social smiles and "sophisticated" conversation, of clammy hands and sleepless nights, of anxiety and triumph and despair.

I remember that it was during the organized suspense of "rushing week" that I discovered the magnificent resources of the library. I penetrated deep into the stacks, relishing the musty smell of books, gaping at the serried ranks of shelves loaded with more books which I wanted to read than any human being could possibly read in a lifetime—let alone in less than four years. And quite by chance I stumbled on Stephen Phillips' verse play, *Francesca da Rimini*. Does anyone remember that palely poetic and youthfully romantic work today? Or even recognize Phillips' name? Probably not. But *Francesca da Rimini* seemed beautiful to me then and I remember thinking to myself as I walked out of the brightly illuminated library into the crisp, cool autumn dusk that even if I failed to be invited to join a fraternity the blow would not be insurmountable. I could be at least adequately happy as long as the library's doors were open and I could find on its shelves unexpected delights like the poetry of Stephen Phillips.

For several nerve-wracking days it looked as if I might have to seek just that sort of consolation. The fraternities wanted athletes, probable leaders of campus organizations and social "smoothies." I obviously didn't fit into any of those categories. But financial necessity forced every fraternity to maintain its quota of dues-paying members by inviting numerous boys who didn't fit into such categories. So there was some ground for hope. My brothers and one of my cousins had belonged to the local chapter of Psi Upsilon, and fraternities set great store by family loyalties.

I was invited to join Psi Upsilon and accepted with alacrity. I never regretted it. Life at Williams without belonging to some fraternity would have been grim indeed. But I found the mystical bonds of fraternal brotherhood as meaningless claptrap as the artificial school spirit at Arnold. And when many years later my son decided that he wanted to go to a university where the fraternity system had been uprooted long ago I encouraged him to do so.

The ideal college fraternity consists of a group of young men eating and living together because they are congenial spirits. Friends will always draw together and form clubs of some kind. Why not do it guided by the inspiration of an old tradition and a national organization? Why not, indeed, if a fraternity were actually much like the ideal? It isn't. A fraternity is organized and kept alive by entirely different and extremely practical considerations. If the future captain of the football team can be induced to join, fine, but the membership must be maintained or there won't be enough money to pay the interest on the mortgage and the cook's salary. So come hell or high water a fixed quota of new members must be pledged each year.

This new group of freshmen is called a delegation. Its members are destined to live together intimately, sharing meals, bedrooms, shower baths, soap, and pajama bottoms. These fellow members of a freshman delegation do not choose each other any more than do convicts in the same cell block. They are chosen by older boys who know them only slightly, some because they are sincerely wanted to bring prestige to the fraternity, many because they are needed and not because they are wanted for themselves. To make rewarding friendships which endure for life within a fraternity is common. But it is always a matter of pure chance. I made two good friends within my delegation and got along amiably with the others. I heartily disliked some of my fraternity brothers in older and younger classes. And I found that the fraternity system cut me off from making many friends outside my own fraternity.

This was not true of the truly gregarious, the easily popular and the "big men on the campus." I am sure that it was true of many, of those who were shy, or reserved, or intellectually independent. There were boys in my class who shared my literary interests, whose company I probably would have enjoyed immensely if I had known who they were or how to become acquainted with them. The existence of several I suspected, but I never knew them well enough to confirm my suspicions. They lived at the other end of the campus and probably would have been as interested as I in finding someone with whom to talk about Shakespeare and the musical glasses.

One of these dim and distant figures has become a distinguished director of plays and motion pictures. One has become a successful writer of popular magazine fiction. Several have become professors of English. Of course, my isolation within my fraternity was largely my own fault. I could have asked anyone I cared to to dinner. But would the dinner have been a happy occasion? I did not think so then. Now I think that the risk was worth taking and if I could relive my college days I would not be so diffident.

In the second half of the 1920's college life had not yet been transformed by the great depression and the wars which followed it. Economics was just one of many subjects offered and not many took it. None of the great fears which have preyed upon the minds of college students for more than twenty-five years troubled us. We were so certain of finding jobs after college that we never gave the matter a thought. Depression was a word we had barely heard of. Fascism was Mussolini's quaint idea in Italy and Nazism was unknown. Communism was a Russian problem and no concern of ours. The last great war had been fought and the Army was only a powerful football team. College students were young in heart then as they have never been since. And intellectually and emotionally most of them were younger than the students of today. The grim possibilities of the modern world drive the young toward a precocious maturity, while in the 1920's most young men clung to their youth as long as possible.

Those were the days of the rumble seat and the raccoon skin coat, of the pocket flask and flopping galoshes, all of them immortalized in the cartoons of John Held, Jr. They were probably no more prevalent at Williams than anywhere else, but they were certainly characteristic of Williams during that era of the fashionable and "gentlemanly C." High marks were not necessarily evidence of eccentricity and undue effort, but they conferred no campus distinction. That was won by popularity, the friendship of the "right" people, social poise, and the ability to speak with easy familiarity about New York speakeasies, famous jazz bands, the latest Follies or Vanities and the most admired girls at Smith and Vassar. Scott Fitzgerald was by no means as widely read by college boys as some modern critics mistakenly suppose. He did express, however, an ideal prevalent in many Eastern colleges when he spoke admiringly of one of his callow young heroes "who casually

attended Yale." Quite a few young men casually attended Williams, too.

Such self-consciously sophisticated youths were the "smoothies." At the opposite end of the collegiate social scale were the "drips" and "wet smacks." These were the boys who wore ill-fitting clothes, whose faces were pimply, whose manners were gauche, who danced badly, if at all, and who studied too ostentatiously. Midway between the two extremes I went my independent way, not so much by deliberate choice as by accident. I was too reserved and much too obsessed by books to be a "smoothie." In fact, the "smoothies" often amused me. They tried so hard to live up to their pretensions! But I was too mature and too familiar with current fashions in ideas, clothes and social behavior to be a genuine "drip."

When I was at Williams chapel attendance was compulsory. Services were held every week-day morning at seven forty-five, with the first class of the day beginning at eight. On Sundays there was a full service with hymns, prayers, a collection and a sermon at eleven in the morning and a short vesper service in the late afternoon. A few cuts were allowed, but not many. Most of the students bitterly resented compulsory chapel attendance and regarded the seven forty-five services with particular fury. If they had no class until eleven they still had to be present. It was a prostitution of religion, the more articulate complained, making worship a means of discipline, little more than an alarm clock to drag boys out of bed.

In my four years at Williams I never knew anybody who went to chapel in a reverent spirit. Some of the undergraduates must have done so, but they were a small minority. Bored and resentful boys studied and slept in chapel and cut it as often as they dared. Attendance was taken by seniors, and it was not easy for freshmen to be absent more often than their officially permitted cuts. But seniors rarely turned in the names of their absent friends and fellow classmates. Consequently, most seniors cut with joyful abandon. In my last year I hardly went to chapel at all.

During freshman and sophomore year athletics were compulsory. This was no hardship in the autumn and spring when I played golf. But the winter term was a prolonged ordeal with a variety of gruesome perils to be endured in the college gymnasium and swimming pool. There three times a week a non-athlete was confronted with a series of harrowing demands, that he perform impossible acrobatics on a wooden horse, that he jump over an impossibly high bar, that he climb an unclimbable rope (all made the more humiliating by the ease with which a few boys did the acrobatics, soared over the bar and flew up the rope). That such public demonstrations of incapacity were good for the soul is theoretically possible. Whether they were of much benefit to the body is more problematical.

In many an autobiography and in countless autobiographical novels, college education is described as a tremendously exciting experience. It was less than that for me. I had been excited about books and ideas for too many years before I entered college. So I wasn't overwhelmed by the prospect of new countries of the mind opening out before me. But I did find many of my courses stimulating and immensely interesting, several a matter of indifference, and two or three raging bores.

To fulfill the requirements for graduation I had to take physics and biology (unbelievably dreary to my non-scientific mind), one more year of Latin and two more of French. I took as many courses in English literature as I could and garnished them with a smattering of philosophy, religion and history. Although several of my professors were brilliant and all my professors and instructors knew their subjects, not all were competent to teach.

Remembering my various teachers and noticing the reactions of my children to theirs, I have concluded that there are three essential requirements for successful teaching: an attractive personality, spontaneous interest in young people and enjoyment of their company, and adequate knowledge of the subject. To expect to find many teachers with all three requirements in as poorly rewarded a profession as theirs would be naïvely unrealistic. When all three do come together in a teacher, his students are fortunate indeed.

A good teacher becomes one because the idea of teaching itself attracts him. But all too many men and women become teachers only because of their interest in the subject, or, worse still, only because they hope that teaching will be an easy way to earn a living. The teachers' colleges which train the majority of our public school teachers are depressing institutions; at least, the half dozen or more where I have lectured seemed so to me. The students were a dismally unprepossessing lot. Several of the college presidents freely admitted to me that so much time is devoted to courses in how to teach, in educational theory and in administrative methods, that the students who graduate to teach other students are not properly educated themselves. Many of them are unaware of their deficiencies or don't care. The girls hope that they will only have to teach a few years, until they marry. The boys are frightened by the hazards of a competitive society and are looking for job security, even if poorly paid. These unfavorable impressions do not apply, of course, to all students at teachers' colleges, only to a number I met personally.

On the college level, of course, the emphasis on post-graduate degrees eliminates all such inadequately educated individuals; but it often fosters the scholar at the expense of the teacher, the man who devotes his life to learning all there is to be known about some trivially small segment of knowledge. I remember one such teacher I had at Williams, a short, stocky solemn young man who had burrowed so deeply into an obscure corner of sixteenth-century literature that he knew more about the poems of George Gascoigne than he did about the novels of Dickens. He taught a course in sixteenth-century literature: More, Wyatt, Sidney, Spenser, Marlowe and Shakespeare. And he taught it as if he were bored to extinction by the necessity of introducing such worthies to unappreciative college boys.

With his head buried in his notebook, never raising his eyes to glance at his anesthetized students, droning along with no perceptible changes in the inflection of his voice, he would read a passage from Shakespeare and then a passage from his notes. The somnolent hum of his voice gave no warning of the change and only one or two particularly wakeful students would realize that the genius had left off and the drudge had taken over. Yet this dull and dreary man, as I later discovered, loved sixteenth-century literature with passion. His trouble was that he had no interest in teaching it to the young. It was my lot to have this bemused scholar as my tutor when I did honors work in English during my junior year.

I chose the English novel as my subject, and Mr. Webb had few suggestions to offer. The field was enormous. He knew a great deal about Sidney's *Arcadia* but little about *Lord Jim*. I explained that I had read many English novels, but that I hoped to fill in the gaps in my reading during this course. That was agreeable with Mr. Webb, who recommended several forerunners of the novel, *The Unfortunate Traveller, Oroonoko* and *Caleb Williams*. He left the rest to me, and I chose books by Scott, Bulwer-Lytton, Dickens, Thackeray, George Eliot and others which I thought it my duty to read.

The only other student who shared my honors class was amenable and followed along with no objections to my choosing most of his reading matter for the year. The system worked beautifully. Mr. Webb began the year by giving us C's on our book reports. But we explained to him that we were A students and never deserved less. He saw his mistake and we received A's thereafter. A strange man!

If Mr. Webb was as uninspiring as a teacher could be without making a full-time project of it, George Burwell Dutton was the reverse, a teacher of superlative brilliance. Short, with a round moon face and pale blue eyes which gleamed and snapped through rimless glasses, he used to walk to class with a load of books in a shabby green bag, limping awkwardly because of a permanently injured foot. The acknowledged star of the English department, Professor Dutton made English literature seem so exciting that students competed for the pleasure and honor of enrolling in his classes. There was a magnetic quality about his enthusiasm for books and for ideas which struck sparks from many a student's mind. His learning was immense but without a trace of pedantry. His lectures were the most extraordinary I have ever heard.

Sitting stiffly erect behind his desk, beaming at his class as if he would rather lecture to it than anything he could dream of, Professor Dutton would begin to speak. Words and sentences of glittering polish and challenging intellectual depth poured from him without a pause. With never a hesitation, with never a glance at a note, he would deliver thoughts of striking originality and subtlety expressed in such beautiful, formal and elaborately constructed sentences that I frequently held my breath while I waited to see if they would come out neatly. They always did. His prose in extemporaneous speech had a rhythmic roll, a balance and wit, an elegance and polish, which made me want to burst into hearty applause after every lecture.

There was nothing synthetic about Professor Dutton's performance. He never stooped to the easy satisfaction of fishing for laughs with tired jokes. He was always intent on the trail of independent thought about literature, ideas and life. The intellectual excitement Professor Dutton provided won him the affectionate admiration of his students, who were fascinated by the spectacle of seeing his brilliant mind drive to the heart of an idea, ruthlessly exposing the shoddy, clearly analyzing a technique or a point of view, generously praising achievements of many kinds. His standards were exacting; he demanded and generally got conscientious work. He expected his students to think for themselves and never rewarded a mere rehash of his own ideas (one of the most common of pedagogical sins). He gave everything he had to his classroom lectures and did not encourage casual social relations. He was the only great teacher I ever knew.

Professor Dutton died early in December, 1930, at the age of forty-nine. His death was a heavy blow to Williams College and a cause of sincere grief to hundreds of Williams men, who, although they had never known him intimately, would never forget what he had done to awaken their minds and to increase their ability to understand and to enjoy the infinite riches of the written word.

Although I profited from the instruction of a number of other able teachers at Williams, there was only one other who seems to me worth recalling now. He was Sherwood Owen Dickerman, Lawrence Professor of Greek Language and Literature, a little gray man with softly twinkling eyes and a gentle smile of irresistible charm. It was his melancholy fate to see fewer and fewer students register for courses in his beloved Greek, but he bore his disappointment with cheerful resignation. And he must have been encouraged to some extent by the enormous popularity of a course he taught in Greek literature in English translation. To him it must have been a second-best. It was a good second-best.

Judged solely by its substance, I now believe that this was the most valuable course I took at Williams. I would have read most of the material required in my various English courses on my own initiative; but without the necessity of keeping up with Professor Dickerman's course in Greek literature, it would have been perilously easy to remain ignorant of much of the greatest and most profoundly influential writing in world literature. It is possible to become acquainted with Greek literature through the study of other subjects, history, drama, philosophy. But to read the Greek classics one after another in the order of their composition is especially stimulating. Only in such fashion can one link them together and form some conception of the culture of which they were so noble an expression.

Professor Dickerman brought to his students a deep and simple love for Greek literature which was both touching and contagious. His gentle humor, his emotional response to the woes of Priam or to the girlish charm of Nausicaa, his delight in the tragic splendors of Sophocles and

Euripides and the enthusiasm with which he read Greek poetry in the original Greek, unintelligible to us but still beautiful, all made his classes unforgettable. His pleasure in introducing students to the great Greek works he loved was so genuine and heart-warming that one could not help but love them too. A good teacher and a good man, he also died in the autumn of 1930, a fateful season for Williams College.

Most college students go to college because it is the conventional custom of their social group. They don't stop to ask why they go. They just go. If persistently pressed to give a reason, they are usually baffled and are likely to resort to remarks which show that they have never given the matter a thought. "Everyone goes." "You need to go to college to get a good job." "My family expects me to." "What would I do if I didn't go to college?"

Until the present century higher education was the privilege of a few. In the classic ages of Greece and Rome it was the private pleasure of the aristocracy. In the Middle Ages it was functional and was intended to train priests, doctors and lawyers, and it has never lost that function. But sometime in the seventeenth century higher education began to seem a desirable ingredient in the training of a cultivated gentleman. It was definitely aristocratic and served the interests of a leisured, ruling class, training future national leaders in Latin and Greek and the history and culture of Rome and Greece. The advantages of this system were primarily, but not exclusively, cultural. They were also ethical. Schoolboys who cut their intellectual eyeteeth on Plutarch and Livy and the ancient philosophers were well grounded in the Stoic virtues. And the practical advantages were not to be overlooked. Latin tags did wonders to dress up a public speech. And a minimum familiarity with Horace and Virgil seemed almost to guarantee an adequate facility in the writing of decent English. But a classical education, in spite of such pleasant perquisites, was an ornamental decoration to the good life and had no deliberate utilitarian purpose.

With the phenomenal increase of public-supported education and the democratization of colleges and universities in the twentieth century, classical education has almost disappeared. And cultural education for its own sake, for the sake of cultivating the individual, is itself on the defensive. Many students have no notion of what kind of education they want. All they want is the cachet of a degree.

In the midst of this confusion one can hear the voices of prophets shouting hoarsely with supreme confidence that the only education worth consideration is one that would meet the approval of St. Thomas Aquinas; while others equally assertive bellow that in the age of the hydrogen bomb and the guided missile a technically scientific education is the only kind fit for serious patriots. Such extremists represent the lunatic fringe of education.

More likely to undermine the very foundations of higher education are the thousands, perhaps millions, who ask two profoundly disturbing questions. These are: What good is education if it is not a useful, preliminary step toward getting a job? And should not education in a democracy be geared to the abilities of the average student, who may be unprepared for genuine higher education because of poor training in secondary schools and lack of cultural incentives in his family surroundings?

These questions are disturbing not because they are pertinent, but because they are so often and so sincerely asked. The first question is a polite way of joining the modern clamor for vocational education. The only answer to the advocates of "practical," vocational education is to remind them as patiently as possible that they are confusing colleges and universities with trade schools and post-graduate schools. The two kinds of educational institutions are not competitive and their purposes are not similar. The student who wants to learn how to become an electric welder can do so in a trade school. The student who wants to practice law or medicine must learn how in a post-graduate school. But the liberal arts college is not concerned with the teaching of professional skills. It is organized and operated with a different goal in view: to help students be more interesting company for themselves and others for the rest of their lives by acquainting them with their heritage as human beings, the great story of what men have done and failed to do, what they have thought, discovered, written and achieved. In the process of learning something about this heritage, the superior student often learns how to think for himself and becomes a better individual and a better citizen. His four years in college is the supreme opportunity of his life for maximum intellectual growth. And, ironically enough, such a non-utilitarian education actually does help get a better job. College degrees are now so common that the lack of one can be a serious handicap to ambitious young people.

The second question is a polite way of demanding that higher education be reduced to the level of the intellectual lowest common denominator. "Everyone ought to have the same chance for a college education," some people parrot without considering the implications of such a statement. Certainly, everyone capable of benefiting from a college education ought to have the chance, and that ideal state has not yet been reached, although we are approaching nearer to it with every generation. But such an ideal is not the same thing by a long shot as the fatuous notion that college education should be degraded until it is within the capabilities of everyone. Everyone is not capable of acquiring a high-school education and some are not capable of passing the first grade. In the last analysis, higher education is an intellectual discipline for people who want to exercise their minds. And many people are unable or unwilling to use their minds and much prefer using their bodies.

This, of course, is natural and right. Any healthy society includes highly educated scientists and scholars and many more less educated persons who are willing to perform the essential and monotonous labors which keep society a going concern. If by some miracle everyone was smart enough to be a nuclear physicist or a professor of aesthetics, and no one was willing to slaughter steers, dig ditches and clean streets, civilization would collapse. Democracy in education means that the opportunity for higher education should be extended to as many of those who can take proper advantage of it as possible, not that a tawdry mockery of higher education be made available to those who would be happier without it and are only made unhappy by exposure to an intellectual climate they cannot understand or endure. Civilizations are created and maintained by an active and responsible minority of able and fortunate persons. This minority in a democracy like ours is fluid and constantly changing and is recruited from all levels of society. Most members of this creative minority are educated in colleges today. Elementary education is available to all, and a host of scholarships make higher education available to many of the exceptionally able who otherwise would be denied it. Many more such scholarships would be desirable. But it is essential that we maintain colleges and universities capable of stimulating the minds and taxing the abilities of our finest young minds. Up to the present we have done so.

The future of education depends upon the freedom of schools and colleges to teach the truth as many individual teachers of unlike minds see the truth, on their freedom to experiment in subject matter and teaching method, on their freedom to represent minority views and to defend unpopular opinions. Such freedoms require that there shall be private schools as well as public schools. The private schools are not always better than the public schools, but they often are, and the standards they uphold serve as a challenge and an inspiration to the public schools. Some prominent persons who should know better have demanded that private schools be eliminated in the name of democracy. Such regimentation would help to eliminate democracy instead, for certainly a desirable democratic freedom is the freedom to send one's children to private school if one believes that they will benefit by it.

One of the sad little jokes current among college professors for generations is the statement that you can expose a student to education but you cannot make sure that it will take. This has always been true. We all know graduates of distinguished institutions who seem unbelievably ignorant, aggressively uninterested in ideas, topical issues or the arts. Many of them are uncritical and enthusiastic conformists with whatever social pattern happens to surround them. Often they are honorable individuals and frequently they are shrewd in their pursuit of an honest profit. But they show no signs of their right to be numbered "in the company of educated men." Their education did not take.

Neither, of course, does all of anyone's. I can remember precious little of my college course in physics, and my present hazy ideas about the subject are based upon newspaper and magazine articles. But I shall never forget the expression on the professor's face after his first lecture on electricity when he asked if there were any questions and I asked him to define electricity. My attention must have wandered, for I hadn't yet grasped the fact that electricity is a mystery known only in the manifestations of its force and cannot be defined. I can't remember either much of what I once learned in my biology course about the anatomy of worms, nor the various provisos of the Peace of Utrecht, nor much of Kant's reasoning about the categorical imperative.

But I shall never forget many of the books I read in college and many of the exciting ideas I first encountered there. I shall never forget the dignity and patient resignation of the bearded scholar who taught Christian philosophy and medieval Catholicism; nor the long hours spent in the library stacks in a dusky quiet broken only occasionally by the rustle of papers or the soft tread of a student padding to the corner where he kept his private pile of books on Oliver Cromwell or Henry James; nor the light streaming through the stained glass windows of the beautiful Gothic chapel on a winter evening; nor the cold blast of night blowing into a rumble seat coming back from Smith on the Mohawk trail; nor the foolishness and fun of a crowd of tipsy students gathered in Patsy's speakeasy in Hoosick Falls.

It was at Williams that I read through the novels of Jane Austen in a rosy glow of delighted admiration; that I first discovered the greatness of Joseph Conrad as a literary artist and as a melancholy interpreter of man's character and fate; that I took an honors course in my senior year devoted solely to Henry Adams and Henry James and discovered the fascination for modern minds of those strange and gifted men who seem somehow more representative of our time than of their own. When I was studying them, of course, no one foresaw that their fashionable revival would reach its present grossly inflated proportions.

And it was at Williams that I wrote poems and short stories which were regularly printed in the college literary magazine of which I was an editor. I have written neither poetry nor fiction since; but it was exciting to write poems and stories then and to see them actually in print. In the autumn of my senior year the stock market collapsed, an event of some interest to read about in the New York *World* but not a matter of much immediate concern in our remote and beautiful Berkshire valley. I only began to realize what that crash meant a year later in the autumn of 1930, after I had spent the summer traveling in Europe with my college roommate. I couldn't find a job.

· seven ·

In the peaceful and prosperous 1920's few college undergraduates worried about what they would do after graduation. I was not one of the few who did. All I knew was that
I didn't want to be a conventional businessman, that I
loved books and knew a good deal about them and that I
liked to write. So, like thousands of other English honor
students before and since, I decided I would like a job in
book publishing. In the Easter vacation of my senior year
I went to New York armed with a letter of introduction
given me by a kind gentleman in the wholesale book
distributing business whose son was a fraternity brother
of mine. The letter worked like a charm and I obtained
brief and coolly polite interviews with some twenty publishers. All pointed out that there was a depression and
that people were being fired, not hired. No one asked me
to drop in again after I graduated in June.

So that was that and I postponed the evil hour of job
hunting until after I returned from my summer trip to
Europe. Back home in Cleveland the local newspapers
and advertising agencies had no pressing need for my services. The depression was nearly a year old by then and the

hatches were being battened down. My father obtained an interview for me with a friend of his who was vice-president of The Cleveland Trust Company, a huge and alarmingly august financial institution.

I knew very well that I didn't want to be a banker and that in no circumstances could I possibly be a good one (I always get a numb feeling in the brain when confronted by figures). But ordinary courtesy to my father and to the vice-president required that I show up for the interview. I did and was greeted by the appalling question: "What makes you think that you would like to be a banker?" I hadn't said that I would like to be a banker, only that if there were a humble job somewhere I would be grateful for a chance at it.

For a momentous interval, while the vice-president smiled at me, I hesitated. And then I told him the truth, that I didn't want to be a banker, that I was just conscientiously trying to find any kind of job I could in that dismal autumn of 1930. The vice-president, knowing well that I didn't need a job in a bank in order to live, smiled approval of such frankness, patted me on the back and ushered me out of his office at once.

After that, since I seemed to be running out of ideas myself, my father produced another one. Many business leaders, he pointed out to me, had started their careers as secretarial assistants to other business leaders. I didn't want to be a business leader, but that was neither here nor there. I did want some kind of honorable employment and the chance while I worked to write and see what might come of my efforts. But my father refused to allow me to change the subject and continued. To be a secretarial assistant, he said, it was needful to know shorthand and double-entry bookkeeping. So off I went in October, 1930, to the Cleveland Business School and one of the oddest experiences of my life.

I was twenty-four years old, a cum laude college graduate with special honors in English, a traveled young man who considered himself thoroughly adult and moderately sophisticated. And I was taking courses in shorthand, typing (I had been a rapid and competent typist for eight years), penmanship and double-entry bookkeeping. My fellow students were boys and girls of seventeen and eighteen, just out of high school, most of them excited about the fraternities and sororities of the business school. The whole situation seemed to me faintly absurd.

For four months I endured this strange interlude as patiently as I could, and then in March, 1931, an escape route suddenly opened before me. A man named J. W. Cooperson, who had formerly been the managing editor of a defunct society magazine in St. Louis, was about to launch a Cleveland magazine which would continue the glorious tradition of its St. Louis predecessor and go on to bigger and better things. He needed a general editorial assistant who would work for little or nothing. I jumped at the chance.

At first it was for little and before we had run our course it was for nothing. But for a year and a half I was up to my ears in every kind of magazine journalism, and I enjoyed every minute of it so thoroughly that I had no complaints. Cooperson himself was an education in the ways of the world. Short, dapper and foxy, he bustled and boasted as if he were the E. W. Scripps of the society magazine business. He told cheerful and enormous lies about our circulation, which never exceeded three or four thousand. He ran up debts and dodged creditors. He reviewed such plays as dared the road in the depths of the depression with the confidence of George Jean Nathan, but with little knowledge of the theatre and only adequate ability to write. And finally, in the autumn of 1932, he saw his leaky craft sink beneath him. For several months we had not been paid our minuscule salaries. Suddenly the long-suffering printer rebelled and demanded cash, and that was the end of poor Cooperson's new and improved society magazine.

Our predecessor in Cleveland, a magazine called *Town Topics,* had enjoyed a long and profitable career until a dearth of advertising in the first years of the depression finished it off. There was no conceivable reason to think that we could succeed in a more severe stage of the depression. Whether Cooperson actually believed that he could perform so improbable a feat I often doubted. At any rate, he hired the elderly lady who had compiled the social notes for the *Town Topics,* a bookkeeper, a woman to sell subscriptions, an old man to sell advertising, a stenographer and myself, and was in business.

Our offices were in the old Caxton Building on Huron just west of East Ninth Street. There I wrote a weekly column of book reviews, a weekly column of art news and criticism, a weekly column on golf, numerous feature articles and interviews and countless picture captions. I checked proof, collected pictures of brides and engaged girls from photographers, answered the phone and even swept the floor. I signed the book reviews with my initials. I didn't dare sign the art column, and left it anonymous. And Cooperson insisted that I sign the golf column "Bill Prescott," feeling that my family nickname was more appropriate for a sports column than my real name.

No publisher, of course, would waste review copies on a publication as obscure as ours. So I made an arrangement with Harry Korner, the beloved dean of Cleveland book-sellers, to let me read books before their publication dates. He used to wrap them in brown paper so I would not soil their jackets and I would return them to him unsullied. I had ample space and was on my own. Cooperson, my only superior, was not interested enough or qualified in any way to make suggestions. I reviewed two or three books a week, reading them in the evening.

The art column was more of a problem. There was a course in art appreciation at Williams, but I hadn't taken it. But I had spent many happy hours in the great galleries of Europe. I knew what I liked, but I also knew enough not to say so very often—I was too aware of how little I knew about modern art, to say nothing about technique. So as a matter of common sense and elementary caution I devoted most of my columns to mere news announcements, what was on view where, and only dipped my toes in the boiling water of art criticism in the most gingerly and tentative fashion.

I used to drive to work in a little Ford coupé and park it a block from our office for ten cents a day. On Mondays I made the rounds of art galleries, the shops and stores which made any pretense of holding picture exhibitions, and the Cleveland Museum of Art. There were tricks to the trade. Some weeks the only legitimate art news was at the museum, where there was usually some new acquisition or some new display to be counted on. But at some of the shops there was no turnover for months at a time. The proprietor and I would consult together about which slow-selling items in his permanent stock he would put on display that week. These would then be called a showing worthy of magazine coverage.

The golf column was more fun. No one who has not

been a golf reporter has any notion of how much golf activity there is near any large city from May to October. City tournaments, regional tournaments, exhibition matches by touring professional stars, inter-club matches, women's events and junior events—they go on continuously and often simultaneously. In the line of duty I learned the location of every golf course in the Cleveland area and managed to play on many of them.

Whenever I drove out to cover a golf event I took my own golf clubs safely locked up in the luggage compartment of my Ford. Sometime in the late afternoon the tournament or exhibition match would be over and the course would be free. And then the members of the press, who by providing publicity helped sell tickets, were allowed to play. This was strictly unofficial, a matter of connivance rather than of formal invitation. I learned about this happy situation from the golf reporter of the Cleveland *News,* a friendly and helpful gentleman who invited me to play with him. I was properly grateful for his aid in initiating me into so pleasant a secret of our profession. But he earned even more profound gratitude when he taught me how to report a golf tournament without nearly killing myself running back and forth across some five miles of hilly countryside.

Except for the Tour de France bicycle race, which lasts more than a week, and mountain-climbing assaults on the more inaccessible peaks of the Himalayas, golf is the most difficult of all sports to watch. A good grandstand seat is all you need for most games. But it takes nearer four hours than three to follow one golf match. And if you do, what are you going to do about the others which are going on at the same time?

The secret is not to waste time and effort following

any one match. The experienced golf reporter picks himself a strategic spot, preferably in the shade and on a slight elevation where he can watch the green of one hole and the tee of the next. There he reposes at his ease, taking mental snapshots of the appearance and mannerisms of the players as they go by. The favorites he can follow for a few holes and then abandon, always returning to his command post. The final scores can be picked up at the club house where they are posted by the officials.

And if anything sensational takes place, such as the National Open champion being defeated by a local boy only fifteen years old, there will always be news of it sweeping through the crowd. Sometimes you can even hire an unemployed caddy to scout for you and report back with flash news items. In 1931 you could hire a small boy to run back and forth across a golf course all afternoon for fifty cents. The price is undoubtedly somewhat higher today.

My desk at the magazine office was just inside the railing which separated an eight-foot square by the door from the space where the stenographer, the advertising salesman and I worked. One afternoon when I was furiously writing winged words about the bright lemon-colored gloves worn by George von Elm, the 1931 runner-up in the National Open who had just made an exhibition appearance at the Canterbury Club, I was disturbed by a sepulchral voice asking, "Are you a writer?"

I paused to consider this difficult question. I certainly hoped to be a writer some day. Even then I was being paid for writing, not much, it was true, and not regularly. But was I entitled to that noble word, writer? Probably not, if one took a long historical view. But in the opinion of the strange creature who leaned over the railing and glared at me with hypnotic intensity, I decided that I was. "Yes," I answered. "That's what I'm doing right now, writing."

The man on the other side of the railing was young, about my own age, shabby, with long, greasy black hair which he wore parted in the middle and which he allowed to hang down well over his ears. His face was a sickly gray, his eyes bloodshot, his manner twitchy. He stared at me grimly for a long minute, shot a suspicious look at the stenographer to make sure that she was not listening, and then said, "I have committed a murder and you are going to write my story for me. It'll be the most terrible story ever written."

Stark incredulity was my first reaction. This cannot be happening to me, I thought, in the office of a society magazine of all places! Why should this creepy character come to me? My visitor opened the little gate in the railing, drew up the only spare chair in our part of the office and sat down beside me in a confidential and conspiratorial manner. He leaned forward and put a bony and dirty hand on my knee. He smelled. "You and I," he said, "are going to be rich. We'll split the profits fifty-fifty. I'll tell you my story and you'll write it. There's never been anything like it. I'd write it myself, only I can't write. But I've got a title for it, 'I Am a Murderer.' Like it?"

"Why did you come here?" I asked. "Do you know who I am?"

"Your name's Prescott, isn't it? A reporter at the *News* sent me. I didn't know where to find a writer. So I went to the paper. He said everyone there was too busy to write my story, but that you were a very talented young writer without enough to do [I winced] and would jump at a chance like this to get into the big money.

"You won't lose by it," he went on. "My story's got everything, big-shot gangsters, hot women, dope and a perfect murder. I tell you no one has even suspected me. Think of it, the murderer's own story when the police don't even know a murder was committed! All the other murderers whose stories you've read in the papers were dopes who got caught."

Was he really a murderer? Or was he insane? Or both? I didn't know then and I don't know yet. But I was certain of one thing. I didn't want to have anything to do with this twitching monster whose presence so close to me sent shivers galloping up and down my spine. Very funny, sending him to me, very funny indeed!

"Look," I said. "I'm the wrong man for you. I'm young and inexperienced. This is my first job. If I wrote your story we probably couldn't get it published. I haven't time to write it anyway. And probably no editor would believe it. They'd think it was a hoax."

"Hoax," he shouted. "I'll show you how much of a hoax I am." Cooperson opened the door of his private office a few inches and peeked out. The stenographer hadn't done any typing since my visitor entered. Her cheerful, round face was strained with her effort not to miss a word. "Do you think I'm a liar? Do you think I'd take the trouble to come in here and talk to you about my murder if I hadn't done it? Do you doubt my word?" He pushed his blinking eyes and protruding lips within a few inches of my face. "I'll, I'll . . ."

"Please don't misunderstand me," I said placatingly. "Of course I believe you. It's the editors, not me, who'll think your story is a hoax. They'll think I made it up myself. And as I told you before, I'm too busy with my job. I haven't time to write it. I couldn't do a good job anyway.

I couldn't possibly write that kind of book. But I'll tell you what I'll do. I'll give you the name of a much better writer than I am. Star reporter over on the *Plain Dealer*. Knows lots about murder. You try him."

The argument lasted a long time, but neither of us had any new points to make. Eventually he left and I felt miserably guilty. But I knew why the *News* man had sent our mysterious stranger to me. It was the only way to get rid of him. I never saw him again. But every now and then I still worry about him. Should I have called the police?

Although the depression and lack of advertising were reasons enough for the dismal failure of Cooperson's reincarnated society magazine, there was another reason. Even if it had been a wonderful magazine, there was no place for it. The world had changed. Readers who cared about society notes and what the bride and her mother wore could still find that sort of information in the newspapers without bothering with us to get a more authoritative and more detailed description of the wedding.

As for our other departments, local news with a society flavor, sports, the various columns I wrote—the newspapers covered such matters better than we could. "Where's their loyalty?" Cooperson complained. "No loyalty, that's the trouble with this damn city. You'd think people would be grateful for what I'm trying to do, maintain standards, uphold traditions. A magazine like mine ought to be subsidized by some wealthy old dame as a civic obligation." But in 1931 and 1932 nobody agreed with him. Nobody cared if the magazine survived or perished. The world was a serious place and there was no room in it for the pale ghost of a defunct society magazine.

But while we tottered along to our predestined and ignominious end I was enjoying myself. I was a working journalist, a magazine writer and a critic. I learned proof-readers' marks and how to set up a dummy page and how to make corrections from the type itself on the printer's stone. I learned to write fast in a small room with the phone ringing, the typewriters clattering and several people shouting furiously at each other. I met people: artists so humble that they were grateful for a brief mention in my column; champion professional golfers who would talk a minute or two in the locker room to a group of local reporters of whom I was the least important and the least conspicuous; restaurant proprietors who invited me and a girl friend to a free dinner in return for a little publicity; visiting celebrities and odd local characters.

I worked fifty hours a week in the office or out on assignments and nine or ten hours extra reading books for my review column. It never occurred to me that I was overworked by all the enlightened standards which would soon be regulating working hours. That I was lucky, I knew and was grateful. I was accumulating a file of clippings of my work. A batch of these actually got me an interview at *Vanity Fair* and I traveled all the way to New York and met Frank Crowenshield and Clare Booth Luce, who were polite but not encouraging. After all, *Vanity Fair* was expiring from lack of advertising nourishment, too.

I was not only lucky because I had a job which I found stimulating and fun at a time when so many people had no jobs at all. I was also fortunate because I did not really need the job. My parents continued to live as they always had. My mother and aunts still maintained Winden unchanged, and we all continued to spend summers there, my aunts in the Big House and the Prescotts in their cottages.

There were only five of us now. The elder of my brothers had married and was living in New York. My other brother was divorced and once again living with the rest of us. My sister had graduated from Smith and was working in a decorator's shop. The house on Fairmount Boulevard was more full of life than it had been at any time since my brothers first went away to preparatory school. And there were six automobiles in the garages, my father's, my mother's, my sister's, my brother's and mine, and an old one used by the yardman and part-time chauffeur to fetch vegetables and flowers from Winden and for other errands. There were five adults in that household, all leading their own lives and all citizens of the automobile age.

Earlier in these pages I mentioned that I do not believe that childhood or school days or college are the best and happiest years. For those favored by the gods, who are destined to take pride and pleasure in their work and to know the abiding joys of a happy marriage, no earlier experiences can rival those of middle-age. But in a different way, there is an intense and almost tingling exhilaration and delight in the years of one's first job which no other time can equal.

Then one feels like an adult and responsible citizen part of the time, and like a confident and irresponsible youth the rest of the time. The compulsion to be successful, the pressure for some noticeable achievement which our society imposes, still rests lightly on one's shoulders. Nobody expects to accomplish much in his early or middle twenties, although occasionally somebody does. New and exciting experiences lie around every corner and enchanting, unexplored vistas beckon from every direction. There are so many kinds of girls, and each kind requires investigation. People are fascinating, odd and full of surprises. Liquor, even Prohibition gin mixed the night before in the bathroom wash bowl, has such amusing possibilities. No wife and children by their mere existence demand serious planning for the future. The future itself seems blissfully remote. And the knowledge in the back of one's mind that this delightful interval of gay suspension between youth and maturity will not last more than another year or two adds to its zest.

Some people, the sour ones who think that life is to be endured rather than lived, may say that to have enjoyed one's first job and the pleasures of being young in the depths of the depression was heartless. I don't think it was. No one in 1931 could ignore the depression. I was reminded of it daily, by every newspaper I read, by scores of books and magazine articles, by the memory of the jobs I had been unable to get, by the poignant problems of some of my friends, and by the fear and misery in the faces of many people. Like millions of others who had grown up in a supposedly secure and peaceful world, I was shocked and alarmed to find that it was neither secure nor peaceful. I read up on politics and economics and worried much about them. But at twenty-four and twenty-five I could not worry all the time.

I found time to play golf regularly every Saturday and Sunday, something I have never had time to do since that summer of 1932. Even now I am tempted to write an essay on the pleasures of not playing golf very well but just well enough. To play golf well requires better muscular coordination than I have ever possessed and a competitive determination to excel in sports which I have never had. When I broke 90 I was delighted. When I failed to do so, which was most of the time, and even when I failed to break 100, I did not grieve unduly. Such an attitude will never get a golfer anywhere. Constant practice is essential. And anyone as physically lazy as I am finds hitting golf balls off a practice tee too dull to tolerate.

I found time to cultivate my friendships with several girls. And I made a cursory investigation of the speakeasy situation in Cleveland. Unlike New York, where many blocks were occupied almost exclusively by speakeasies, there was no particular district in Cleveland devoted to the sale and consumption of illegal drinks—or if there was I never found it. There was only one speakeasy with an elaborate décor, fine food and famous entertainers, but that was a gambling joint, too, and I never went there. If there were others I did not hear of them. But I found two places which I remember with considerable pleasure.

One was a "club" which occupied several enormous rooms in the cellar of a warehouse on the West Side, which is on the other side of the Cuyahoga River, and is Cleveland's equivalent of Brooklyn. It was organized by a community of Germans and was dedicated to the proposition that beer was a civilized drink which didn't have to be as frightful as most Prohibition homemade brew or gangster-supplied suds. In some Cleveland speakeasies the beer was bright red and tasted like shoe polish. At the club, it looked like beer, tasted like beer and was only needled enough to speak with authority. Huge steaks smothered in onions and French fried potatoes were the other leading attractions. These and the club's staid and respectable family atmosphere made it an ideal destination for boys and girls out for an evening in groups.

But when I wanted to talk seriously to a girl about Life I would take her to dinner at another "club." It also occupied a cellar, a small one in the East Nineties, a residential district which had once been pleasantly middle-class but which had fallen on evil days. The proprietor was dark, smiling, bespectacled and polite. He insisted on seemly behavior and refused to serve drinks to any customer who in his judgment had reached his capacity. His cook was quite good. Somehow he always managed to make his unpretentious bar and restaurant seem cozy and genial and friendly and hospitable. He didn't serve beer. But his whiskey was good as bootleg whiskey went. At least, it never inflicted injury graver than a reasonable hangover.

Hundreds of thousands of words have been written about the delights of the speakeasy age, most of them completely unjustified. The truth of the matter is that most speakeasies served mediocre drinks for ridiculously high prices in unattractive quarters. All, of course, were illegal. Some were operated more or less honestly by decent men and women who only wanted to earn a living in a traditional fashion which most of mankind has always thought honorable. Since many speakeasies, however, were operated by thugs and gangsters, customers could rarely be sure which kind they were patronizing.

The men and women who write about speakeasies with tears in their eyes and sobs in their throats do so for two reasons. One is that they remember the pleasing excitement involved in defying a monstrously stupid law by drinking poor liquor in grubby surroundings. After all, they were responsible citizens and they were breaking the law of the land. But the law was such an outrageous invasion of privacy, such a dictatorial attempt to regulate personal habits to suit the prejudices of a bigoted minority, that they felt morally justified, almost like crusaders, in defying it—a fine sensation.

The second reason why some writers have written sentimental gush about speakeasies is that they were young when they patronized them and they are no longer young.

It was youth and youth alone which added an atmosphere of gaiety and charm to the speakeasies of the late 1920's and early 1930's, a charm which was entirely subjective and was born of the customers' own minds. The hills were higher, the pastures greener, and the speakeasies glamorous long ago when we were young.

After the final total collapse of our tottering magazine in September, 1932, I was jobless again for nearly four months. My next job brought me to New York in the week between Christmas of 1932 and New Year's Day of 1933.

· eight ·

Two days after Christmas, 1932, I took the New York Central train for New York at the East Cleveland suburban station. Like many thousands of young men and women before me (and after me, also) I was lured to the American metropolis like a cat to a fish market. There, I was convinced, was opportunity, culture, intellectual stimulation and urban sophistication. A job in New York, no matter how humble, would be exciting in itself and might open a gateway to unknown and fascinating possibilities. What future was there for a young man with literary tastes in Cleveland? I knew, of course, that I could achieve a great future in Cleveland or anywhere else if my literary abilities were as genuine as my literary tastes. I knew well that they were not; yet I was determined to make some kind of writing my work. More magazine journalism seemed to be the answer.

By the greatest good fortune, when I boarded the train on that cold, windy winter evening, I was not setting out in the trough of the depression to hunt for a New York job. I had one. For this I was properly grateful, but I was extremely apprehensive nevertheless. I wanted to live and work and write in New York; but my desire to do so was thoroughly mixed with clammy self-doubts.

New York was the big league and I was only a rookie granted a crucial tryout. It was New York which drew to itself so many of the nation's able and ambitious young men and smiled on so few of them. New York was the arena where the battle for success was fought more desperately than anywhere else. In New York the modern cult of cold careerism flourished more rankly and competition reached a higher peak of ruthlessness than anywhere else. As the train rocked along toward Buffalo I brooded on these truths and found no comfort in them.

Recently I had been reading the *Meditations* of Marcus Aurelius, attracted to the noble stoicism of the great emperor by a need for the consolations of philosophy. A beautiful, brilliant and extraordinarily nice girl and I had reached the parting of our ways after a deliriously happy interval during which we had contemplated never parting at all. This disaster had plunged me into an abyss of gloom. But my abrupt descent from rapturous heights to morose depths had not prevented me from reacting in a typically bookish fashion. Surely there could be no more appropriate reading for a man whose love was blighted than Marcus Aurelius. Hadn't he said that "very little is needed to make a happy life"? For several months I had been telling myself that so commonplace a grief as mine should not make me as unhappy as it did.

Marcus Aurelius had said that very little was enough, and I had so much. He would have had small patience with my worries about New York. Didn't I have a job waiting for me? Didn't I have a fine home and devoted parents to fall back upon if I made a mess of the job? Wasn't I young and healthy, with the pangs of love already much abated? What more did I want?

When I walked up the ramp into the Grand Central station the next morning my eldest brother was waiting for me at the gate. He was the only man in New York I knew well enough to speak to if I should meet him on the street. He took me to the Williams Club, arranged a guest card so that I could live there until I became a member, too, and then went off to his work in the paint business. I had nothing to do until January second, when I was due to report for work, except explore New York.

On January 2, 1933, much too early in the morning (New York working hours begin at least an hour later than Cleveland working hours), I walked into the first, temporary offices of *Newsweek* magazine as a member of the original editorial staff of a publication which did not yet exist. This miracle was the result of a fateful lunch in the Statler Hotel in Cleveland several months before. My host was a newspaperman from New York. He was preparing to launch a new magazine and was making a tour, promoting his venture, raising funds and hiring a staff. A friend of a friend of a friend had suggested that we meet. Thomas J. C. Martin, a short, round-headed man with bright blue eyes, was a *New York Times* alumnus. His new magazine would be a news weekly, like *Time,* only different and better.

Next to my earning that five-dollar gold piece by learning to read, that luncheon was the most momentous event of my life. Because of it I came to New York and became a literary journalist. Because of it I met the girl who became my wife. When the luncheon was over I had a job with *Newsweek.* That much was clear and definite. But, I discovered later, there had not been a complete meeting of minds. A slight misunderstanding only, it was explained to me in New York.

I had thought that I was hired for $25 a week and that my principal job would be writing book reviews. Now $25 was hardly munificent, even in 1933; but it went a lot further then than it would today and was not bad considering the prevailing wages of beginners in journalism at that time. But my first pay check wasn't for $25; it was for $20.

I wasn't going to write book reviews. I was going to be a researcher assigned to get background material for articles on science, medicine and the press. Since a foothold, no matter how precarious, in New York journalism in 1933 was more precious than rubies, I knew better than to protest. But the situation did seem rather odd. My employer knew that my education had been as exclusively literary as I could make it and that I knew nothing whatever about science and medicine. I had already proved that I could write competent magazine journalism. Nevertheless, I was made a scientific expert and given a job where I wrote only rarely for publication.

My situation was not unique. Round pegs in square holes were so common in the first feverish days of *Newsweek* that they caused no comment. Tommy Martin, the publisher, was so burdened by the horrendous problems involved in launching a new national magazine at the most unpropitious moment, psychologically and economically speaking, in the twentieth century that he had no time to be an editorial executive. The editor, Samuel Williamson, also a *New York Times* alumnus, was an able newspaperman, a smooth and even charming writer when he had time to write smoothly and charmingly, an amiable, kind and likable person. But Sam Williamson had not chosen all the members of his staff, and some were oddly chosen indeed.

To be a researcher and theoretical expert on subjects about which you know nothing is difficult, but not quite so difficult as one might at first think. The trick is to obtain authentic information from people who can speak with authority, or from printed sources. My immediate superior, who wrote the articles on science, medicine and the press for which I dug up background information, was a graduate of Massachusetts Institute of Technology, who had discovered that he had more of a flair for journalism than for applied science. He was vaguely familiar with many matters which were unfathomable mysteries to me; but he was not professionally expert about any branch of science or medicine. His specialty was breathless journalese. No matter how technical and dull the medical research which was the news of the moment, Jack would write about it with panting excitement and many an imaginary flourish.

"Look," I would say. "We don't know how Dr. von Eberstadt felt when the white rat came out all over spots. You have no right to say that he felt weak in the stomach and broke into a sweat of excitement. Maybe he took it calmly. This is meant to be a news magazine."

Jack would lean back in his swivel chair with an air of oh-God-give-me-patience and explain the facts of journalistic life to me. "Bill, have I said that anything happened to that damn rat which didn't? Have I said that Dr. von Eberstadt claims he can now cure cancer or polio? Well, then, the medical facts are right. But medical facts are dull. Readers want human interest. I dress up the facts with a little legitimate human interest and you squeal like a stuck pig. What do you think I'm hired to do, write like a doctor preparing a paper to be read at the A.M.A. convention?"

Of course, journalistically speaking, he was right and I was wrong. But we researchers were officially responsible for the accuracy of every word in our superiors' stories. I never did outgrow my nervousness over Jack's high-pressure prose and fanciful embroidery work.

To keep up with the news in science, medicine and the press Jack and I read dozens of newspapers, many general magazines and dozens of technical journals. If a new treatment for leprosy was being tried out in the Philippine Islands and there was nothing else of medical news interest, that would be our story. If we could find out little about the new treatment, most of our story would be about leprosy. And that was where my life became complicated.

In the New York Public Library I would read up on leprosy in the back files of magazines. Much of this material was useful and could be rehashed. But it wasn't gruesome enough. So I would go into exile in the great medical library of the New York Academy of Medicine and track down the most grisly facts about leprosy that medical textbooks and medical journals contained. No matter what the disease, I would read about its symptoms, prevalence, past history, current mortality rate, methods of treatment, its famous victims and the doctors, if any, who had won fame in fighting it.

Now, medical literature is written in a technical vocabulary which medical students spend years in mastering. To understand even a reasonable amount of what I read, I always had to have a medical dictionary beside me as I took notes. It was a laborious process. I often spent several days a week in the Academy library patiently collecting masses of information which Jack would later condense into one or two vivid and gruesome paragraphs. It was dull and tiresome work, and could have been done better and more quickly by anyone with a natural bent toward scientific writing and some initial interest in the technical background of medical research.

Considerably more interesting was the direct reporting which frequently came my way. If a doctor, scientist or newspaper man broke into the news and could be tracked down in the New York metropolitan area, I would be assigned to interview him. This was not always easy to do, because many doctors shunned publicity, and even when cornered, answered questions in grumpy, technical monosyllables. Others would refuse point-blank to be interviewed and I would have to do the best I could while I had them on the other end of a telephone wire. To satisfy Jack's fetish for personal touches, I would find myself in the embarrassing position of asking some distinguished winner of the Nobel Prize to describe his private emotions and to tell me the color of his eyes.

The national conventions were more fun. In my official capacity I attended conventions of surgeons, internists, pediatricians, obstetricians, ophthalmologists, opticians, homeopathists, osteopaths, chiropractors and veterinarians. I collected so many free samples that if I had saved them I could have set myself up as a quack doctor. I admired brightly colored charts of diseased organs, listened to learned papers I could not understand, and collected mimeographed copies for Jack's later study. The scientists caused me even more trouble than the doctors. There were fewer of them in New York and they usually held their conventions elsewhere. So I rarely could ask direct questions and had to struggle with the printed sources, most of which were in special libraries similar to the medical library.

In my freshman year at college I had flunked physics and had had to repeat it the next year. No wonder, then, that I did not have to venture far from shore before nearly drowning in deep waters. On numerous occasions I had to admit defeat and, like the elephant's child, confess that this was too much for me. If the atomic age had dawned in 1935 instead of in 1945, it would not have made much difference to me. I was used to scientific mysteries I could not understand. It would only have been one more.

Our articles about the press caused me much less trouble and interested me much more. We covered the births and deaths of magazines and newspapers, major changes of policy and of personnel, significant anniversaries, the winning of prizes, strikes and the early days of the Newspaper Guild. I interviewed celebrities: Floyd Gibbons, Heywood Broun, George McManus, Pulitzer Prize winners, publishers, editors, reporters, the crackpot founders of fascist publications and the fanatical employees of communist publications. All this I could do with some feeling of professional competence, a wonderful sensation compared with my usual condition of abject humility when confronted by the baffling mysteries of medicine and science.

The preceding paragraphs sound as if my years at *Newsweek* were frantically busy. They weren't really. They were frantically busy in spurts. Often I had only routine and humble tasks to perform, clipping newspapers and reading copy for typing errors or errors of fact. This was so dull and so low on the journalistic ladder—one rung above the cleaning women and the janitors—that I hunted for extra work. For a year I was *Newsweek's* "religious" editor, a title which amused me enormously. I wrote news reports on new churches, new bishops and new controversies, interviewed Jesuit scholars and Oxford group gladhanders, and read denominational publications, which are considerably more lively than medical journals.

I had no connection with the magazine's book review department, but the man who conducted it was not overly fond of work and he often let me do one of the three reviews which customarily filled his space. All I got for this extra work in his department was satisfaction, since, like everything else in *Newsweek* then, the reviews were unsigned and I was not paid for them. During those same *Newsweek* years I managed to contribute a few book reviews to other publications, a dozen or more throughout one autumn season to the *Herald Tribune "Books,"* just one to *The New York Times Book Review,* several to obscure magazines which perished long ago and whose names I no longer remember.

Although I had often been in New York before for a few days or a few hours, I found that being a brand-new New Yorker fresh from Ohio was a strange and a quite exhilarating experience. There was so much of everything! So many book shops, so many theatres, so many people! I remember my surprise when I first noticed the cheap eating places where people stood up in rows while they munched hot dogs and hamburgers and drank coffee and orange juice. Standing up for lunch! Imagine it! I remember my excited admiration of the just completed Empire State building; and the worldly pleasure of having dinner once a week in Felix's excellent speakeasy (I ate most of my other meals in one-arm restaurants and cafeterias); and the almost physical impact of the depression.

In Cleveland the depression had been terrifying enough; but it had not seemed so close. There I drove to work and back again in my little Ford and saw much less of the life of the streets than in New York, where I was always walking somewhere on my assignments for *Newsweek* or on expeditions of my own. And the New York streets were pitiful. Everywhere were beggars and apple-sellers and the pinched, drawn faces of the bewildered victims of a disaster that even the economists could not understand. In Columbus Circle the silent, shuffling lines filed up to the free soup kitchens, and in the underground passage which leads past Gimbel's basement to the Long Island Railroad station a dozen men slept on the pavement every night with newspapers wrapped around them beneath their shabby jackets. No one knew when it would end. No one guessed that, although the various New Deal measures would prove helpful, the depression would not really end until it was defeated by the astronomical expenditures of an even worse disaster, war and the continuing threat of war.

A more gregarious person than I would have found my life in those first few months of 1933 unbearably lonely and would have taken steps to remedy matters. But I was not consciously lonely. I borrowed Turgenev's *Smoke* and *A Nest of Gentlefolk* from the Public Library at Fifth Avenue and Forty-second Street, where I spent so many of my working hours, and read them at night in my little room in the Williams Club. I went to the movies occasionally and to the theatre every now and then. In 1933 one could walk up to the box office of any hit and buy tickets with no trouble at all. And one could get a three-course luncheon at Madame Raffier's with soup and filet of sole and two vegetables and French bread and biscuit tortoni for only forty-five cents.

In March I moved from the Williams Club to a four-room apartment on Wadsworth Avenue in Washington

Heights. This migration to the far north of Manhattan came about because my college roommate, with whom I had gone to Europe in the summer after our graduation, was a medical student at the Columbia College of Physicians and Surgeons and wished to live nearer his base of operations than at his family home in Westchester County. He found the apartment, but it was too large and too expensive for one. It was just right and very cheap for two. Not least among its attractions, Ches pointed out, was the presence in the apartment across the landing of four sprightly student nurses.

Never did two young bachelors begin housekeeping in a state of such sublime innocence. We went to a five-and-ten-cent store and solemnly equipped our kitchen with a tea kettle, a skillet, a cooking pot, a kitchen knife, four plates, four cups and saucers, four forks, knives and spoons, a large kitchen spoon, an orange squeezer, a spatula and four tumblers. In a grocery store we bought bread, butter, sugar, salt, oranges, milk, coffee, eggs and bacon. We couldn't think of anything else we might need for light housekeeping. After all, we were only planning on cooking breakfasts. Time enough to worry about other kinds of food when we gave our first dinner party, which we hoped would be soon.

Although our apartment was meagerly furnished and was definitely dismal in appearance, our first party, with all four of the nurses as our guests, was a triumphant success. We mixed cocktails according to a recipe I had discovered in one of those drink-mixing guides which bloomed as Prohibition tottered to its predestined end. The recipe required the use of a great deal of cream.

We cooked ham and eggs and boiled beets. We put the beets on to boil ten minutes before we planned to eat them. We knew no better and neither did any of the nurses. Naturally, the beets were as hard as golf balls and we couldn't imagine why. Finally, in desperation I telephoned a Cleveland girl I knew who had recently moved to New York and asked her if she had ever cooked beets. She hadn't, but she thought she remembered hearing somewhere how it was done. Ten minutes' boiling wasn't enough. Two hours was nearer the proper time. Needless to say, all this was before the invention of that boon to civilized man, the pressure cooker.

It wasn't until we had lived happily in our new home for six weeks that we realized we had neglected to equip it completely. Something didn't seem just right. The air was always stuffy and our footprints showed in the hall. Maybe we ought to get someone to do a little light cleaning. Although I worked on a five-day, two-nights-until-the-small-hours schedule, I was free on Tuesdays and Wednesdays, and the cleaning issue was squarely up to me. So bright and early one Wednesday morning I went to a domestic employment agency a few blocks away and announced that I wanted to hire a cleaning woman. Nothing could be easier. In two minutes I was walking back to our apartment escorting a large and friendly colored woman. "It's a trifle dusty, I'm afraid," I said. "But I'm sure that you won't have any trouble putting everything right."

"Dusty!" she said. "It looks like a pigpen. When did you last clean up around here?" Since the only cleaning we had done in six weeks was to wipe the ring out of the bathtub, that was an embarrassing question. But there was too much evidence for deceit to be possible. "We never have cleaned up," I admitted. "Oh, well," she said, "you're young and don't know no better. Now just show me where the mop and broom and Dutch Cleanser and dusting cloths are and I'll get going." Mop? Broom? Dutch Cleanser? What had they to do with either the study of medicine or the pursuit of a literary career?

"Look," I said, "you write down a list of everything you need to clean up with, and while I run out to the hardware store, you can just sit here and read until I get back." That was fine with Judy. But when it turned out that we had no copy of the New York *Daily Mirror,* only one of Turgenev's *A Lear of the Steppes,* Judy decided that she didn't feel much like reading after all. She'd just sit and rest her feet until I returned with the necessary equipment. From then on, until I gave up bachelor housekeeping the following November, Judy came to us once a week and by her heroic efforts kept the flag of civilization flying in the dreary, dark apartment we called home.

In 1933 *Newsweek's* offices were on the eighteenth floor of the RKO Building in Radio City. During my first few weeks there, I was so busy learning the ropes of a new job and charting a path through the general confusion that I was slow in getting acquainted with my fellow employees. But one day when I went out for lunch I found that I shared the elevator with only one other passenger, Miss Ward-Smith, the researcher for the business and financial news department. She was a short, slight girl with a perky manner and an appealing smile. It seemed silly to stand there without speaking to her, and to speak to her and then rush off to a lonely lunch by myself seemed sillier still. I asked her if she were free and would care to lunch with me. She was and would. As we crossed Fiftieth Street I asked what her first name was. "Lilias," she said. "What?" I exclaimed, hesitating in the middle of the street and nearly getting run over by a crosstown bus. I had never heard that name before.

We ate lunch in a cheap cafeteria and enjoyed the occasion. Lilias had graduated from Smith and was a classmate of my sister's. She had worked briefly at Macy's and Lord and Taylor's and for the Reconstruction Finance Corporation. In spite of this last impressive-sounding connection, she knew no more about business, banking and the stock market than I did about medicine and science. That's the way jobs were parceled out at *Newsweek* in those days.

A day or two later Lilias came into the office carrying a book which she had been reading on the commuting train from Garden City. It was a novel by Virginia Woolf. This obviously required looking into. I invited her to go to dinner and the theatre with me. She accepted. One thing led to another and soon we were in the habit of lunching together whenever our research assignments did not make it impossible.

And then one day the book Lilias was carrying back and forth with her was *War and Peace*. That would never do. I had read other books by Tolstoy and a good selection of Dostoevsky and Turgenev, but never *War and Peace*. What a situation! I hastened to repair that gap in my education at once. As time went on it seemed to be necessary to see Lilias more and more often outside of office hours, to spend some of our middle-of-the-week weekends visiting at her home on Long Island, playing golf and swimming together. Early in June we became engaged. And on November first in the beautiful Episcopal cathedral in Garden City we were married. Our combined salaries made the grand total of $40 a week. Fortunately, my allowance from my family supplemented that sum sufficiently so that we could start life together in a three-room apartment on East Forty-eighth Street.

Since this book is not a romantic novel about marriage (much less an intimately psychological one!), I am not going to attempt to characterize my wife or to describe our life together in detail. All I can bring myself to say is that because of Lilias' extraordinary combination of character, intelligence and charm, my life has been blessed beyond my deserts and far beyond the reasonable expectation of any fallible male.

· *nine* ·

The middle 1930's in New York and in most other parts
of the civilized world was a strange, a sad and a bitterly
controversial time. The air was dark with the smoke of
burning issues. Everywhere the continual din of voices
raised in furious debate sounded in one's ears. Were the
political and economic experiments of the New Deal
needed reforms and practical steps taken to alleviate
misery? Or were they part of a deliberate effort to change
the very nature of our society and government? And if
they were, was the effort noble in purpose or a sinister
conspiracy? Were fascism and nazism unspeakable abominations, or was there something to be said for them? Was
communism only a radical reform movement, or was it a
threat to free men everywhere? What about WPA, war in
Ethiopia, TVA, civil war in Spain, AAA, and war in Man-
churia and China?

To most of these questions history has given unequiv-
ocal answers. All of them are too familiar to require analysis in as personal a narrative as this. But in the middle
1930's I was a working journalist. As the fateful drama
of contemporary history mounted from climax to climax,

each more portentous than the last, my absorption in the gruesome spectacle deepened. I could not fail to note the portents in the sky, nor fail to hear the doleful voices prophesying war. I could not fail to take sides and to hold strong opinions.

My principal interests were bookish, with a slight inclination toward an ivory tower if I could find one in a good neighborhood at a modest rental. My usual reaction to public events was skeptical pessimism tempered by hope and by allegiance to the cause of individual freedom. Such proclivities did not prevent my feeling the necessity of deciding for myself where I stood on the clamorous issues of my time. No one without the mind of a worm and the spinal column of a jelly fish could wish to avoid doing that.

In 1932 I voted for Roosevelt, feeling that we desperately needed a change from the Hoover administration's palsied clutch on crucial affairs. In 1936, in spite of some troublesome qualms and doubts, I voted for Roosevelt again. It just wasn't possible to vote for an innocuous nonentity like Landon. And besides, I sincerely admired the zeal, if not all the methods, with which Roosevelt sought to help the victims of depression.

Many of the New Deal reforms seemed to me to be admirable. But the New Deal determinedly fostered the growth of federal power as if that were a desirable end in itself and involved the state in innumerable activities which were undeniably socialistic. This was entirely in conformity with a worldwide trend toward the welfare state and probably nothing much can be done about it. Nevertheless, the world trend seems to me to be dangerous.

The trend reflects a popular conviction that governments are not only more powerful than their citizens, but that they are wiser and are responsible for their economic security and should take care of them "from the cradle to the grave." It assumes that government officials should be entrusted with enormous power over the economic life of the people as well as over their political life. It assumes that this power will be wisely used by honorable and benevolent men. Now, even among the few politicians who are well informed about economics, there is no agreement about economics. Senator Harry Byrd does not see eye to eye with Senator Paul Douglas.

Most politicians know little about economics. And most are far more concerned with their political ambitions than with the economic welfare of the country as a whole. The vastly increased political power of the state is alarming enough without granting it equal power over our jobs, our businesses, our incomes and our savings. Politicians are not equipped to exercise such power wisely. Neither, in all probability, are economists who differ with one another as a matter of principle.

The fantastic complexities of modern civilization seem to require many new functions of government. But it seems to be only normal caution and common sense to grant each new function with reluctance and suspicion, to postpone each new function as long as possible, and to remember that every new government employee ceases to be a productive member of our society and becomes an additional drain upon the rest of us.

The cruel dilemma of our time is that in a world of warring hemispheres powerful governments are necessary, and powerful governments are always a threat to the liberties of their citizens. And always we should remember that most of the men who achieve power in a powerful government seek it because they like power, not because they are wise and benevolent. And the men who like power the most are the unscrupulous demagogues.

Such men have often governed our states and disgraced the floor of our Senate. So far they have not attained the presidency. But we cannot count on great presidents like Lincoln, or even on able presidents like Franklin Roosevelt, who, with all his grievous faults, was an idealist and a patriot. We are likely enough to put weak men in the White House, like Harding. In a time of crisis we might easily elect a dangerous demagogue, like Huey Long. It should be almost axiomatic that the less power available for such men to misuse, no matter what office they hold, the better for us all.

Therefore, holding these opinions, as 1940 approached I decided that further tinkering with our system of government would be a mistake. So the last two times Roosevelt ran I voted against him. To vote for him twice and against him twice seemed perfectly reasonable to me, but it didn't to all my Democratic and Republican friends. And, of course, there is always the likelihood that I was acting in an entirely conventional and predictable manner, growing more conservative as I grew older.

Whenever we feel our political opinions solidifying into an unbreakable mold, it would be a good idea to remind ourselves that our politics are never half so reasonable or so disinterestedly intelligent as we think. More than on anything else they are based upon our notions (often misguided) of our economic self-interest. We think that we are thinking about abstract principles and the good of the nation when in reality we are thinking about our pocketbooks.

A manufacturer wants a high tariff to protect his indus-

try and votes Republican because Republicans traditionally approve higher tariffs than Democrats. But lower tariffs or no tariffs at all might in the long run help the manufacturer. Or they might ruin him. Authorities differ and
no one can be sure. Few politicians dare advocate free trade
today and no nation dares return to it.

A farmer voting for a representative pledged to support high parity prices on excess crops is voting cash into
his pocket. But he is also voting for a policy of subsidizing
a particular section of the population at the expense of
the whole population. How long such a policy will continue to benefit the farmer, how far it will spread to other,
competing sections of the population, and whether it will
generate a catastrophic general dependence on government handouts, no man can tell.

What is certain is that economics is not yet a science
understood by everyone. It is still a study of imponderable
factors and of unpredictable circumstances. Its students
know much more than they did a hundred or even fifty
years ago. But they still don't know enough to assume the
awful responsibility for the welfare of us all. They still
are vulnerable to the familiar American retort discourte-
ous, "If you're so smart why ain't you rich?"

Next to ideas of economic self-interest, pure emotion is
the most important molder of political opinion. Political
emotion can be regional and hereditary, like Democratic
feeling in Alabama and Republican fervor in Vermont. It
can also be an outward expression of optimism and ideal-
ism, or of pessimism and skepticism. And it can reflect
basic attributes of character.

No man ever became a convinced fascist who did not
crave the security and exclusive merit of belonging to
something, who did not rejoice at the prospect of being

united with his comrades in brotherly hatred of others. I doubt if any man ever became a communist for as logical reasons as he thought. Belief in communism, I am convinced, is an act of faith in direct contradiction of the evidence, a surrender of the individual will to the authority of an irrational organization which promises more pie in the sky than has ever been promised before, but pie only to be reached after marching in lockstep through rivers of blood.

According to one definition, politics is the art of the possible. That's from the point of view of the politician. But from the point of view of the average citizen, politics is the actual operation of government in society. And most people aren't really interested in the operation of government, only in its results. As long as most of us leave the operation of government to the professionals whose interest is in jobs and power, it is ridiculous for anyone to be surprised or shocked by political stupidity, inefficiency or corruption. Such things are human and inevitable. They are worse in some countries than in others, for as a general rule we do get the governments we deserve—except, of course, when governments are imposed and maintained by force.

The wonder of American politics is not how bad but how good they are. It is really amazing that we don't have more Pendergasts and Hagues, more Huey Longs and Boss Tweeds. Most of our politicians may present no inspiring sight. But somehow we always have with us a minority of able and comparatively disinterested men and a few distinguished men.

Our particular variety of political democracy may wobble and flounder, its faults may stink in the nostrils of the righteous; but so far it has worked. There may be no such thing as a really good and efficient system of government. But a two-party democracy is the freest and best which has yet been tried and found reasonably adequate by any sizable segment of mankind.

Returning to the middle thirties and the politics then breaking out all over, I remember that I detested both fascism and communism as soon as I became aware of them. In 1927 in Italy I had ridden on Mussolini's trains, which ran more or less on time, but I was not as impressed as I was by a Roman taxi driver who spoke excellent English and was afraid to discuss Mussolini with American tourists. I had followed the rise of Hitler in newspapers, magazines and books and had no illusions about the monstrous nature of that half-demented enemy of the human race.

So I was all the more shocked and astonished one evening when Lilias and I were dining with friends. The evening was thoroughly enjoyable until the conversation turned to Hitler and the Nazis. Our host spoke up. He had recently made a short business trip to Germany and had been there all of two weeks. Consequently, he knew far more about conditions there than could anyone who only relied upon the superb foreign news coverage of *The New York Times*.

I was all wrong to denounce Hitler, he said. Hitler was just what Germany needed. He'd done wonders for her. Business was on its feet again. Unemployment abolished. Communists on the run. Persecution of the Jews was greatly exaggerated. He knew. He hadn't seen a single atrocity all the time he'd been in Germany. There was nothing I could say. We said good night and never saw our host again. Four years later we learned he had been killed fighting in the American Army.

Sympathy with the Nazis was never widespread in the

United States, in spite of the best efforts of the German American Bund, the Silver Shirts and similar crackpot organizations. But my wife and I encountered one manifestation of American fascism which was odd indeed. One evening in 1935 (or maybe in 1934) we went to a cocktail party. The party was small and memorably dull. But it was unusual because half the young men present wore identical gray shirts of a military cut. I sought enlightenment. The shirts, our hostess said, were just another of Virgil's notions.

Virgil is the name I have given to a talented dilettante of several arts who had not yet "found himself." But now he believed that he had. He had recently returned from Louisiana, where he had conducted his own private survey of the local dictatorship of Huey Long. His close-up view of the Kingfish in action and his admiration for Mussolini and Hitler had filled Virgil with a determination to imitate their inspiring examples. In New York he had founded his own fascist party. He himself was its fuehrer, and a considerable percentage of its membership was present at the cocktail party. Somewhat later Virgil was to turn up in Germany as a guest of Goering.

If Virgil's folly had not been so sickening it would have been funny. His foray into fascism was as short-lived as it was ludicrous. Nothing came of his revolting antics. But the fact that this highly educated and fortunate young man, a young man with plenty of money and very considerable talents which have since won him success and fame, should even dream of aping Hitler was a symptom of something terribly wrong within himself. He had no reason to be a fascist revolutionist and, of course, no capacity to be one. What was the nature of his neurotic compulsion, I do not know. Probably it resembled that of other privileged young men who flirted with fascism in the 1930's and the larger number who dabbled in communism.

Tormented by inner insecurities, oppressed by vague feelings of guilt because they lived on inherited wealth and did little or nothing to earn their own keep, excited and confused by the world economic and political crisis, they longed to justify themselves by participating in a conspicuous movement well supplied with slogans, catchwords and cure-alls. That these movements appealed principally to the ignorant and emotionally unstable was no deterrent. They were ignorant about politics and history and they were extremely unstable emotionally. Often they were idealistic, too. They really believed the official nonsense of their parties.

Since I was working in magazine journalism, and by 1937 as a book columnist, I inevitably met a few of the intellectual and literary communists whose influence and numbers have been so grossly exaggerated. But, no doubt because I did not frequent the correct circles, I did not meet many. I remember being sent by *Newsweek* to get some information from one of the important communist publications.

In those days, 1935 or perhaps it was 1936, communists were far from respectable; but the true nature of their evil conspiracy was not nearly so well known as it is today. They were eager for publicity and for converts. While I waited for an official handout, a manifesto, or whatever it was that *Newsweek* wanted, a fat, lumpy young woman in a mustard-colored sweater asked me, "You're a magazine worker, too, aren't you?"

I had to admit that I was. "Are you one of us?" she inquired.

"If you mean am I a communist, I'm not."

"Of, well," she said. "I'm sure you're a fellow traveler, anyway."

It was the first time I had heard the phrase and I didn't like the sound of it. "No," I said with considerable indignation, "I'm not a fellow traveler of yours and I'm not traveling in the same direction as any communist zealot or any befuddled dupe like you." Her mouth dropped open in surprise. Immediately I felt ashamed, for I had been exceedingly rude to a young woman who had been polite to me. The fact that she was ignorant enough and stupid enough to be tricked by the fraudulent blandishments of the communists did not excuse me.

"I'm sorry," I said. "I spoke too hastily. But I believe in freedom and in democracy and in capitalism, and you are the first person who ever assumed that I didn't. I was taken by surprise."

At several small literary parties and several functions held to solicit funds for supposedly worthy but probably questionable causes, I heard literary intellectuals spout the Communist party line. Most of them were so obscure and so lacking in genuine talent that I cannot recall their names. I never joined any of their organizations because I didn't agree with a thing they stood for. I didn't even like their faces. All in all, I probably saw less of the intellectual communists and knew less about them than any literary journalist in New York.

Several of those who honestly believed communism meant reform rather than terror have since seen the error of their ways. And they have written long books explaining with fervor and great moral self-righteousness why they were so deluded. Their explanations may be sincere; but they make remarkably little sense. Although in the 1930's we did not know as much about communism as we do now, the facts were not secret. Communism as an idyllic dream of a new and better way to organize society was obviously unworkable. That it was a totalitarian dictatorship depending for survival in its own country upon terror was obvious, too. We did not realize how frightful that terror was. But there was plenty of evidence that it existed.

In politics as in religion it is the will to believe which counts. Neurotic intellectuals (a very small minority of those who might properly be called intellectuals), unbalanced by their fears and complexes, deeply disturbed by the suffering caused by the depression, yearned for a panacea for their ailments and the world's. They closed their eyes, deliberately refused to see the true nature of the dose they were swallowing, and gulped down communism —bad taste, bad smell and Russian spoon all together.

· ten ·

By 1936 I felt that I had exhausted the possibilities of
my job at *Newsweek,* and I was growing increasingly restless every week. I was nearly thirty years old. I hadn't got-
ten anywhere. I didn't seem to be in the process of getting
anywhere. It was obvious that there was no future for me
in doing medical and scientific research. I had no gift for it
and no taste for it either. At any time somebody in authority might have a brain storm and replace me with a
researcher who really knew something about medicine and
science. And I was involved in two personality clashes
which were making life difficult.

In an imperfect world such clashes are inevitable. Some
people are as born to irritate each other as others seem to
be to fall in love. Antagonisms need no logical foundation.
They can flourish merely because two people do not think
alike, because they operate on different wave lengths, because something mysterious in the expression or the tone
of voice of one makes the other's hackles rise in instant hos-
tility. Except for two people, my relations with everyone
at *Newsweek* were amiable; but those two, who regarded
me with suspicion and dislike, outranked me.

If I had been more consistently tactful, if I had kept my mouth shut all the time instead of only most of the time, if I had refrained from showing on several occasions that I thought myself better informed than those two superiors of mine, the situation would have been different, not necessarily better in the long run, but certainly different. But if I could have done all those things I would have been a different young man than I was, more diplomatic and more cautious than I had it in me to be. But I was still young, anxious to excel and much too quick to speak out—not very often, but often enough to do myself no good.

With a little more circumspection and some gross flattery I probably could have remained in the good graces of the elderly newspaperman down on his luck who was nominally in charge of all researchers. But not even the charm of Franklin D. Roosevelt, the diplomacy of Talleyrand and the "humility" of Uriah Heep could have won me the approval of the new managing editor.

Henry Calhoun was a heavy, pompous, morose-looking individual who wore his steel-gray hair in long wings swept back over his ears. He walked with a nervous bounce, sat in an awkward sprawl and talked in a curt, sardonic manner designed to hide his habitual nervous tension. He had worked at editorial jobs on several other magazines before he came to *Newsweek*. He was supposed to coordinate the editorial department, introduce efficiency and brighten up the copy generally, rewriting whenever he thought he could improve it.

Such functions were admirable in theory and if entrusted to the right person. Properly carried out, they would have benefited the magazine. But it was hard to consider Calhoun's editorial capacities objectively because of his personality. Calhoun was rude, domineering and sarcastic. Not one of my favorite people!

And before I realized what kind of man Calhoun was, how dearly he loved a grudge and how persistently he waged a feud, I corrected several of his errors of fact while checking copy for accuracy. This was a major tactical error. But I was not content to make a mistake of tactics. With incredible folly I showed my surprise that Calhoun knew so little as to make such errors. That was lese majesty and unforgivable. Even before the Calhoun regime I had wanted to leave *Newsweek*. Now it seemed absolutely essential that I find a new job.

Fortunately for me, I found one soon. In September, 1936, after three and three-fourths years at *Newsweek,* I resigned. Never again would I have to read about hernias in the Academy of Medicine library. Never again would I have to try to understand how a cyclotron worked, or why a filterable virus is filterable. No longer would I have to walk softly in Henry Calhoun's scowling presence. With a sense of blessed relief I said good-bye to Jack, who was always friendly and pleasant in spite of my lack of enthusiasm for his specialty, and to the other editors and researchers.

My new job was as a member of the editorial staff of a new magazine devoted to the entertainment world of New York. It was called *Cue,* and a friend of my brother's and of mine had recently become its publisher. During the spring and summer of 1936 I had written several articles which *Cue* had published. Now I was going to be a Jack-of-all-editorial-trades again, just as I had been in the old days on the Cleveland society magazine. It was almost like coming home.

Although several writers contributed regular weekly

columns to *Cue* and several people were busily engaged compiling its comprehensive listings of information about the theatre, the movies, restaurants, night clubs and radio, there were only three of us general editors. The editor-in-chief was Jesse Zunser, as agreeable and soft-hearted a man as ever pounded a typewriter in the bedlam of a magazine office. Jesse was also *Cue's* movie critic, a position he still holds. My other editorial colleague was Thomas Brailsford Felder, a young man of social charm and sophisticated wit, whose elegance of dress and manner were delightfully out of keeping with the journalistic climate during the 1930's when social significance and horny-handed politics were the fashion.

For nine months we edited *Cue* with enthusiasm, doing the best we could on an editorial budget so small that we paid contributors only $20 per article, each of us doing everything as the need arose. Once again I fitted advertising and editorial matter together, as I had in Cleveland. And once, when our messenger boy lost our sample dummy on the subway, I went down to the printing shop at the last moment and from memory fitted it together on the printer's stone. I wrote articles, picture captions, many movie reviews and a column of brief reviews of detective novels. This last pursuit I found so depressing that I permanently lost my appetite for detective stories and have only read three or four in the last fifteen years. I also read and edited manuscripts.

Our low rates did not attract many talented contributors. Probably we were not inspired editors. *Cue's* function as a service magazine (all those listings) took precedence anyway. The depression lowered. Distinguished magazines several generations old gave up the struggle and our own newborn infant did not prosper.

Regarding this situation with natural alarm, the publisher decided that drastic steps must be taken. He had no complaints with our services, strenuous and most villainously ill paid. But, he felt, a more experienced editor was needed someone who could take full editorial charge, coordinate our efforts, improve the magazine generally and give it a more distinctive personality. That was fine with Jesse, Tom and me. Anything which helped *Cue* would in the long run help us, too.

Several days later the publisher summoned me to his office to meet our new editor-in-chief. Although my curiosity was great, as was only to be expected, I felt no premonitions of imminent disaster. But when I stepped through the door the earth seemed to lurch under my feet and my stomach twisted into a tight knot. There in a chair at the publisher's right hand, sprawling in his usual fashion and obviously master of the situation, sat Henry Calhoun. At *Newsweek* he had made it painfully clear that he couldn't bear the sight of me, and now he was my boss again at *Cue*. I smiled as politely as I could, but I must have looked as ill as if I had eaten tainted fish. Yes, of course I knew Mr. Calhoun. We had worked together before. And that was that.

A week later, after Calhoun had had time to install himself in his editorial chair and to assume the reins of power, he called me into his office. "Sit down," he said. There was an ominous pause while he glared at me with glum distaste. "What can you do to justify your further employment at *Cue*?" he asked.

That was a stunner. I had done everything which could be done on a magazine, every kind of editorial chore. I had written every kind of copy, including several articles which had aroused talk and favorable comment. Calhoun knew this, but I pointed it out to him as politely and reasonably as I could. He said nothing, stared at me morosely and then announced that from that moment I was not to review any more movies and that the column of detective story reviews was abolished.

During the next few weeks I was told to discontinue every other task I was accustomed to performing. I was left with nothing whatever to do. Then my humble weekly salary was cut off and replaced by an insulting $50 per month. Every day I came to the office ready and anxious to work, and was not allowed to. I wrote long letters, wrote light verse and humorous squibs for other magazines, which did not sell, and sat and worried. The situation was gruesome. Every day I expected my frail, technical connection with the magazine to be severed. But as long as I was not fired, as long as I received a child's pay for no work, I was not going to resign. It is always easier to find a new job if you have one, and during the depressed thirties this truth was even more true than at any other time.

I would come to the office late, after job-hunting, and leave early to hunt jobs. Magazine journalism and books were the only things I knew much about. I applied for jobs at a score of magazines. I wrote to others in other cities. I tried newspapers in New York and in other cities. I enrolled in an employment agency. And I grew so desperate with frustration and rage that I even made a journey to investigate a job as the editor of a non-technical medical magazine!

I do not know if my situation was unique. It certainly was unusual. I did not suffer from the cold and dreadful fear which preyed upon so many millions during the depression. After all, Lilias and I were living in a seven-room apartment on East Eighty-second Street with our two children and with two servants, a cook and a nurse. From nine to five life was tense and exasperating; but the rest of the time it was good. We went regularly to the theatre, to the better movies (especially the French ones), to art galleries, and I was always reading as many of the best current books as I could. But my pride was humiliated daily.

To apply for a job, to fill out forms, to try to make a favorable impression during an interview with someone who may be courteous and pleasant, or who may be bored, patronizing or rude is a nerve-wracking ordeal. "Sell yourself" is the slogan which is handed out for such occasions. But how? I did not know, but I persisted in my attempts and bore the strain with such philosophic patience as I could muster. After all, it was the job in name only which I had that was really fraying my nerves.

At *Cue* I was the target of a campaign of psychological warfare and I could not fight back. The rules of business warfare forbid the underling from taking aggressive action against the boss. Calhoun never spoke to me. He never relented and allowed me to work at the humblest task. I watched my friends and fellow employees scurrying busily from one chore to another, and they watched me with discreet sympathy. Why I was not fired I did not know. But it was obvious that Calhoun was doing his best to force me to quit.

For nearly five months we acted our parts in this peculiar farce. Of course, I could have demanded an explanation from the publisher. But I was too proud. If he knew about the situation, as I suspected he did, he was no longer a friend of mine. If he did not, I was still too proud to complain about my lot to higher authority. It was some cold comfort to know that I could resign at any time. But

I was stubborn. I was damned if I would give Calhoun the satisfaction. As soon as I found another job I would resign with pleasure, but my most promising leads always failed to materialize.

Under the Calhoun regime I was not the only one who chafed beneath the iron rule of the occupation. Other employees were snubbed and insulted. Resentments smoldered and feelings were outraged. One stenographer was actually driven to violent rebellion. She seized a heavy dictionary and brought it down with all her feeble strength on Calhoun's head. The pleasure she derived from this beautiful gesture must have been enormous, but the emotional release was so great that immediately afterward she burst into tears.

If startling improvements had appeared in *Cue's* editorial contents, if the circulation had risen rapidly, or if any significant change for the better could have been credited to the Calhoun regime, much would have been forgiven. Results speak for themselves, and success in a competitive world justifies most methods. But the magazine was not transformed and its staff morale was shattered.

And then one Monday morning I went glumly to my non-work as usual. I arrived late, also as usual, for what was the use of being prompt and having that much more time to spend in conspicuous idleness? Calhoun's office was empty and suspiciously neat. Employees gathered together in little groups buzzed with hopeful speculation. Could it really be true? Had we succeeded in weathering the storm and were we out safely on the other side of the hurricane area? Our suspense did not last long.

The publisher called Jesse, Tom and me into his office and imparted the glad tidings. Henry Calhoun was no longer with us. It had all been a mistake, a well-intentioned effort to forge ahead which hadn't turned out as expected. Other new editors might be hired to do what Calhoun had failed to do. But there would be no more Calhouns. As we were filing out the door, filled with joy and gladness, the publisher called me back. Did I know why Calhoun had never actually fired me? No, I certainly did not. It was plain to me that nothing would have given him more pleasure. It was a mystery to me. "I told him he couldn't," said the publisher. He had permitted the psychological warfare campaign, but not the shooting war.

A few days later *Cue's* editors, compilers and regular contributors gathered together at a dinner party to celebrate their emancipation from Calhoun's tyranny. They were united, like a band of brothers, by a unanimous emotion of relief and pleasure which required convivial celebration.

Immediately thereafter I was asked to write a book column, a real one, concerned with the best books and not just with detective stories. My first column of concise reviews appeared in *Cue* in November, 1937. I continued to write it for the next ten years, until the autumn of 1947 when the column was dropped because of a change in editorial policy. But long before that, in the spring of 1942, I had ceased to be a member of *Cue's* editorial staff. I had resigned to become a daily book critic on *The New York Times*.

· eleven ·

Sometime in the autumn of 1934 Lilias resigned from her job at *Newsweek*. Early in the morning of July 15, 1935, Peter was born. July fourteenth, I remember, was one of the hottest days expectant parents ever had to endure in impatient waiting. Two years later, on June 7, 1937, Jennifer was born. Both events I found every bit as harrowing as fathers are traditionally supposed to find them. Both, of course, have proved infinitely rewarding. Parenthood is generally well spoken of and needs no endorsement from me.

Nevertheless, I can't forbear repeating that being a father is one of the most interesting experiences that can happen to anyone, the second most interesting of all possible experiences. The first, of course, is being the husband of the woman you love. But the joy of parenthood does not begin as soon for a man as for a woman. A newborn infant seldom charms his emotionally exhausted father. And although a smiling, gurgling baby is cute enough and even moderately appealing, he is by no means so irresistible as all women seem to find him. A child really begins to be interesting only when you can talk to him and he can begin to talk back.

From then on there are certain to be enough pleasures, troubles and complications to hold any sympathetic father's interest. And if the child is not a fiendish brat destined from birth for a future career as a juvenile delinquent, sharing his development and doing what one can to point him in the way one thinks he should go is a joy and a delight. That it is also a grave responsibility a thousand books, articles and lecturers have drummed into the heads of modern parents until some of them are pitifully afraid of their own children, afraid of bruising their tender egos, afraid of imposing the necessary discipline without which the child is likely to grow up a monster of selfishness and uncontrolled emotion.

Even though the importance of infancy and childhood and the influences which mold them has been stressed ad nauseam, many fathers still seem to think as their grandfathers did that bringing up the children is their mother's job. It has to be Mother's more than Daddy's, because in most families Mother stays home and Daddy does not. By the sweat of his brow, the painful exercise of his mind and the agonizing vibration of every nerve in his body, Daddy supports his family. To provide food, clothing, shelter and a shiny new automobile is exhausting. Even so, it isn't the whole of a father's responsibility.

Being a wife, mother, cook, housekeeper, nurse, hostess and officer of the P.T.A. is exhausting, too. In some respects it is more exhausting than an office or factory job. The hours are longer and are filled with more petty decisions and more unexpected crises. Parenthood being a double responsibility, it is better for the children and better for their mother if Daddy recognizes its double nature. If he does not somehow find time to play a major part in his children's lives, if he does not play games with his children and tell stories to them, if he does not actively concern himself with the ideas about conduct, character and religion they are taught, he has neglected his parental duty. He has also missed a valuable experience which forces him to painful thought and brings out the best, and occasionally the worst, he has in him. I did my best to bear my share of raising our children, and enjoyed the experience. Well, I enjoyed most of it.

Our children are nearly grown up now and, for better or worse, our jobs as parents are nearly over. Looking back on our performance, it is easy to see mistakes and probably equally easy not to see other mistakes which are plain to our friends or to the children. But one thing I can claim for their mother and me. We did our best and did not expect other people to be responsible for our children. I hope that such a claim does not sound smug. I make it as a protest against those among my fellow parents who demand that the schools assume the responsibilities which they are too lazy or too indifferent to discharge themselves.

To ask tired, harried and underpaid teachers to become foster parents in addition to all their other duties is an outrageous imposition. Yet parents, who may have legitimate grounds for criticizing schools for their failures in teaching or for their choice of subjects taught, often criticize them instead for not performing the parents' own duties. "I don't know what is the matter with Jimmy's school," some mother complains. "Jimmy speaks the most atrocious English. His manners are terrible. He never reads a book if he can help it. He doesn't know the difference between Noah and Jonah."

Such complaints are absurd. They refer to matters which must be taught in the home if they are to be learned at all. Teachers have all they can conceivably handle teach-

Vasiliu

ing children reading, writing, arithmetic, French and how not to be prejudiced. It is Mother and Daddy who must set a good example in their speech and see that Jimmy follows it. Manners are always a reflection of the daily practices of the family. If Mother and Daddy care about manners they will see that Jimmy acquires them. The process will probably be arduous, because at his age Jimmy can't be expected to care much about manners.

As for reading—the joy of reading and the habit of reading seem to spring into being in a few children by spontaneous combustion. Most children never do learn that books add immeasurably to the pleasures and rewards of life. Of the children who do become readers most do so because Mother and Daddy read aloud to them, set an example by reading to themselves, kept books always at hand as a normal enrichment of life and lured their children on by providing books chosen to appeal to their age and interests.

Noah and Jonah, of course, belong to the special subject of religious instruction. Some exceptional Sunday Schools can take care of this. But in most, well-intentioned amateurs with no special qualifications as teachers or as interpreters of religion do the best they can. It isn't good enough. Whatever your personal religious beliefs, if you care what your children believe on religious subjects—that they know the difference between Noah and Jonah and what were the teachings of Jesus—you had better become another amateur Sunday School teacher yourself. You will make mistakes, but they won't be the mistakes which would irritate you most if others made them. You can make sure that nothing which you believe vital is neglected and you can leave out what you believe to be trivial. Such instruction is a grave responsibility; but it can be a pleasure, too. Devout and orthodox believers ought to enjoy the duty of teaching religion in the home. Unbelievers can enjoy it, too, because the Bible is the most important book in all Western history and because the teachings of Jesus are the most important contribution ever made to our ideals of ethical conduct.

New York, Lilias and I agreed, was a fine place for babies. A baby is not particular and does not object to being wheeled to the park every morning and afternoon. But New York, we were convinced, was no place for children. What kind of a child's life was it when he could never be on his own, away from adult supervision? Children should have a yard to dig in when they feel like digging, a brook to dam and wade in when they feel like damming or wading, and woods and fields to explore when they feel adventurous. And most important of all, they should have roots, a feeling of belonging to a community. So in September, 1939, we moved to Connecticut.

Our migration made us feel quite like typical New Yorkers. Lilias was born in Tennessee and I in Ohio. We had lived in New York for nearly six years after our marriage. And then, "for the sake of the children," in the most orthodox New York fashion, we moved out of New York and settled down in Fairfield County.

· twelve ·

It was only by accident that we settled in the town where we still live. We first studied maps and eliminated one town after another. Several were in communities already too crowded. We had no intention of moving from one apartment house to another. Others wouldn't do because the commuting was inconvenient. We wanted a place which would seem reasonably countrified, but not too rural. We had to be near good schools and not too far from the creature comforts of civilization. Since we were definitely not going back to the land in a pioneer spirit, we chose a community about which we knew nothing whatever except that its location seemed a guarantee that it would meet our requirements.

When we drove out one weekend a real estate agent showed us several houses that wouldn't do at all. The attractive ones had no rooms for children. The practical ones were aggressively unattractive. The real estate agent stared at us in a long look of frank appraisal. Why didn't we try the next town east, he asked. He thought it might be more our kind of place. Without asking him what kind of place he thought suitable for the likes of us, we took him at his word. So-and-so was a reliable real estate agent there, he told us. Within a half-hour we were talking to so-and-so.

As he drove us around the town we realized that it was perfect. Old, charming, with two beautiful white colonial churches overlooking God's Acre (the village green), the village itself was small; but the township sprawled over a considerable area in the traditional manner of New England townships. Originally a farming center, the town had boasted several factories in the nineteenth century. But these, fortunately, had long since disappeared. In the 1890's several wealthy New York families had bought property in the town and built imposing houses. And in the following forty years other families from New York of less wealth (and a few of more) found a haven there also.

They came seeking space and beauty and escape from the noise and dirt and bustle of a big city, just like the many thousands of other families who were fleeing from urban centers all over the country. Individuals acted with personal motives and rarely realized that they were participating in a mass social phenomenon. In our town they bought old farmhouses and remodeled them, but only a few old barns—those cartoons notwithstanding. And they built modest and comfortable houses according to the tastes of the first four decades of this century.

The town grew steadily, but not so rapidly as to cause alarm. The commuters scattered all over the township on winding country roads with quaint names—Buttery Road, Frogtown Road, Father Peter's Lane. Some bought large parcels of land, some small, but all had plenty of space between them and their neighbors. And the townspeople, who included families which had lived continuously in the town for 200 years, looked upon the new arrivals with mixed emotions. They were most definitely outsiders, "off

Islanders" in the Martha's Vineyard sense. But their business in the local shops was welcome. A certain social restraint divides commuters and townspeople still; but this has been surmounted by many individuals who have served together on the same committees and have learned to respect and like each other.

The house we rented was an old New England farmhouse, at least it was when looked at directly from the front. From the sides and rear it was no special kind of house at all, because its owner had more than doubled its size by building additional rooms. The large lawn had been left uncut and the grass was several feet high. The garden was so choked with weeds, it was difficult to be certain just where it was. Day lilies grew thickly along one side of the lawn, like some rank jungle growth. Poison ivy covered crumbling stone walls. A huge willow tree wept at one end of the lawn and two enormous maple trees, far past their normal span of life, guarded the gate in the white picket fence. It was perfect. We stayed there for four years.

When we moved to the country we did not know anybody in the town. But we did have an introduction to one couple. We met neighbors, fellow parents, fellow commuters and people with similar interests. We soon made friends, and from the first weeks never doubted that we had come home. But our only experience as a married couple had been in New York apartments with a handyman on the other end of the house telephone system. We had much to learn.

Trying to light the gas hot-water heater I singed my hair and eyebrows. Confronted with a coal furnace for the first time in my life, I had no notion that it drank water with a camel's thirst in addition to consuming coal. No one had ever told me. Mechanically-minded people who are good with their hands invariably assume that other people know what they know. They assume that sometime in your childhood, probably before your sixth birthday, you were taught all about furnace boilers and electric fuses, all about plumbing and spark plugs and radio tubes. But some of us were never even introduced to such problems. We have to have things explained to us which any child should know. Sometimes we have to have them explained several times, because the subject doesn't really interest us and our attention wanders. Ignorance and inexperience make moving interesting—from an apartment on East Eighty-second Street in New York to a country road in Connecticut with a mule pasture two hundred yards away.

Something about the fields and woods in which we walked, something in the very country air during that historically momentous autumn of 1939, awoke my long dormant love of animals. I remembered Sandy and my canine sleeping companions at Bridger Ranch. Wasn't it obvious that what our family needed was a dog? For the sake of the children if not for ours? Lilias consented, provided we got an Irish setter. In her opinion, and in mine, too, they are the most beautiful of all dogs, and if we had to have a dog she didn't see any reason not to have a beautiful one. So I gave Rufus to Lilias for Christmas and he was the most beautiful dog who ever lived. He was also the most nervously high-strung.

We all loved him and he loved all of us. When he knocked the children down, or snatched their toys away, or backed them up against a wall and licked their faces, he did so only out of exuberant spirits and family feeling. But Rufus didn't like anybody except us, and no one else liked him. Neighbors' children ran home in tears, terrified by his appalling snarls. Delivery boys didn't dare get out of their trucks. We had to meet them in the drive to get the groceries. Gardeners walking to work at the nearby nursery carried sticks and handfuls of stones for self-defense.

I pleaded with them to walk slowly, to speak softly, not to jump up and down and wave their arms, to appeal to Rufus' better nature. He was really a nice dog. But they did not believe me. That lowered head, those bristling hairs, the blood-curdling growl were more persuasive. One sunny June morning as I stood in my underwear with lather on my face, razor in hand, I looked out the bathroom window. Rufus was attacking his favorite enemy, an excitable Italian. Still clutching the razor, I rushed to the rescue, but too late. Rufus met me on the front steps, grinning with pride and pleasure, the seat of the gardener's trousers already deposited on our door mat.

His next trophy was a red and white silk summer dress, badly tattered by the time we discovered it. Resigned to the worst, Lilias sat down at the telephone and called up various neighbors one by one. The search was soon over. Yes, said the little old lady down the road. She was missing a dress from her clothesline. Yes, it was her best dress. No, she wouldn't tell us how much it had cost, but it was her most expensive. We sent her a check, enough for a better dress we were sure, and we beat Rufus while holding his nose to the bedraggled dress.

But animal training did not seem to be one of our skills. Rufus knew who was master in our family. And it wasn't Lilias or I. Another gardener savagely knocked off his bicycle and a cloth coat with a fur collar torn to pieces and strewn around our yard settled the problem. Rufus was beautiful, but he was a wild animal and we didn't know how to tame him. We couldn't give him away in our town.

His reputation was too well established. We had to give him to a kennel man in a town forty miles away. But Rufus was missed. The little old lady met Lilias on the street and smilingly complained, "I haven't had a new dress since Master Rufus left."

It is probably impossible to put into exact words the characteristic quality which distinguishes one commuting community from another. It is easier to say what our town is not than what it is. It is not a suburb in the sense that Larchmont and Englewood and Garden City are suburbs. We are still too countrified for that, too sparsely settled, too horrified by any suggestion of town lots and commercial housing developments. But our country roads are lined with so many houses and the built-up center of the village is spreading so fast that we have little resemblance to genuine country towns like Wilton or Weston or Washington, Connecticut.

For several years now, considerably more than half the husbands in our town have gone to New York daily on the New York, New Haven and Hartford. Some are driven to the station in the morning by their wives and are met there in the evening. More drive themselves and leave their automobiles in parking spaces so crowded that we jostle for position. A few park Jaguars and Cadillacs all day long near the station. More park Buicks and many more still park Chevrolets and Fords, jeeps and ancient jalopies.

Some of our commuters have lived here for thirty years or more. So many came in the great land rush that followed the Second World War, I sometimes catch myself staring at the newcomers with all the surprise of an old settler. A few of the commuters live in lordly houses and collect paintings by Matisse and Rouault. Most live in unpretentious medium-sized to small houses. Most are Republicans, but the Democrats are active, articulate and respected. We don't fight much over politics; but sometimes we lose our tempers over zoning problems or the best site for the new high school.

In certain self-consciously intellectual circles it is fashionable to sneer at a town like ours. Bourgeois commuters, conventional and smug! Some of us are, of course, as is only to be expected. But the average level of brains, talent and accomplishment in our town is extraordinarily high. And the variety of occupations is great. Bankers, brokers, lawyers and advertising men (and particularly advertising men) abound. And so in somewhat less profusion do publishers, novelists, journalists, painters, actors, architects and eccentric putterers.

Some of my neighbors are tycoons who wield great financial and industrial power. Some are mighty men in the world of the theatre, radio and television. One is a ghost writer who with great speed and great competence writes books which other people sign. One is an inventor. And so many are architects of the most extreme modern variety that our town is in some danger of becoming an important tourist attraction. On nearly any of our country roads you are likely to find houses which are glass cubes, houses which have blank brick walls and cantilever porches, houses which look like chicken coops, jails, morgues and twenty-first-century police stations.

These houses disturb the peace of mind of some of our more conservative citizens and they are always good for an argument. But if many of us are unconverted, plenty of us are enthusiastic. The prosperous and middle-aged build modern houses in our town; and so do young couples with five children all under eight years old. This enthusiasm

for an architectural vogue is only a sample of the enthusiasms which boil over into dozens of activities and projects. Busy men return from their work in the city, sip a restorative cocktail, gulp down a hasty dinner and rush off to meetings several evenings a week. They labor with public-spirited zeal on town committees, on fund-raising campaigns for scores of worthy causes, and in groups which investigate matters of public interest such as various forms of local government and the population trends of Fairfield County. They act in our semi-professional little theatre, cultivate amateur hobbies, do research for our historical society. And when the spirit moves them, they write polite, grateful or angry letters to our weekly newspaper.

Our wives are even busier than we are. At least they seem so to us. They are cooks and chauffeurs, gardeners and nurses, house painters and still-life painters, and hobbyists in more diversified fields than their husbands. Some like to square dance, some to compose popular music. Some write books for children and some write books about how to train horses and dogs. Many band together in groups to study this and that, and many are members of the Society for the Advancement, Protection and Preservation of Everything Meritorious. Energetic, capable, charming and nice to look at, the wives of our town are a credit to modern American civilization as well as the pride and joy of their husbands.

In recent years there has been much discussion of the wave of conformity which is supposed to be sweeping over American life. It may be doing that somewhere, but so far it hasn't reached our town. To the extent that most of us came here because this is the kind of town in which we wanted to live, we are alike. Most of us, women as well as men, are college graduates. But we don't think alike and we feel no need to pretend that we do. We do different things for fun as well as for profit. Some like to play bridge, but they don't urge those of us who loathe the game to play it, too. Some read Mickey Spillane. More read the current selections of the Book-of-the-Month Club and the Literary Guild. Some read Santayana and John Donne. Some play golf and tennis with furious concentration and watch baseball and football with dedicated zeal. Many think that they get enough exercise chopping kindling or keeping the grass mowed and haven't seen an organized game of any sort since they graduated from college.

In our town our houses are not very close together and the family living three hundred yards down the road is no more likely to be one's friends than a family five miles away. The result is that we are a friendly community, but not a neighborly one. Gossip takes place over the tea cups and at parties, not over the back yard fence. We do not run in and out of each other's houses to borrow a cup of sugar.

Although our average of education, cultural background and sophistication is extremely high, our genuine highbrows are few. I know several readers of the *Partisan Review* and one reader of a technical philosophical journal. But they are the exceptions. Most of us prefer less specialized magazines, *The Saturday Review, Harper's, The Atlantic, The New Yorker, Time, Life* and *Newsweek*. And this seems to me to be a healthy and desirable situation. Our minority devoted to the avant garde in arts and letters is large enough to keep our conservatives alertly on the defensive.

In a semi-rural predominantly commuting community growing as rapidly as ours there can be no such thing as an hereditary circle of "best families." Friends must be quite close before they know anything about each other's parents. All of us commuters are newcomers to a varying degree and social background is generally unknown and nearly always unimportant. Each individual is judged for himself, mostly whether he is pleasant, agreeable and interesting; a little, perhaps, on what he has accomplished. People find their own level. The town is still small, but it is big enough so that there are many different circles, groups and social subdivisions which meet but do not mix. But they do not mix because they are not particularly congenial, not because there are any rigid social bars.

These remarks probably sound as if I thought that our town was "the next station to heaven" (the slogan on our weekly newspaper). Of course, it isn't. Our town is inhabited by fallible human beings with plenty of faults and troubles of their own as well as their share of the troubles now oppressing Western civilization. It would be possible to compile quite a list of things which are wrong or of people who are unhappy in our town. But I think to do so would be to convey a false impression.

This is a wonderful town in which to live. It may be fiercely untypical, but it is just because it is so special and desirable that I count myself fortunate to be a "long-time resident," as our weekly paper calls people like me. The twentieth century is cursed with violence and sickened with fear. It is torn by political, economic, social and spiritual unrest. These factors condition all our lives. But they rage less loudly in one's ears in our town than in most. One can forget them for a little while and pretend that one is living normally. We might as well live in our tormented present as pleasantly as we can. The pleasantest place to live in that I know of is the small Connecticut town from which I commute three times a week into New York.

· *thirteen* ·

A few days after we had moved to Connecticut, after milk-men from four different companies had presented us with sample bottles of their milk, but before the curtains were up, the lady from the Welcome Wagon called. A Welcome Wagon is a cute name for an advertising device. A gracious neighbor seems to be recommending the best local shops and services out of sheer benevolence. Actually, she is recommending only those which have joined together in a spirit of business exterprise and employed her to "welcome" new families. After our caller had finished her sales talk we talked polite generalities, and in the course of them she discovered that I was the book columnist of *Cue*. She registered surprising enthusiasm. A few weeks later I found out why.

A letter arrived asking if I would be so kind as to deliver a lecture to the members of the women's club. Here was a pretty how-do-you-do. Only once in my life had I spoken in public—on graduation day at Williams, when as class poet I read an alleged poem of my own composition and thanked my guardian angel for the black academic gown which mercifully hid my quaking knees. The very idea was alarming. But we were brand-new settlers and knew nobody. Could I refuse and risk offending many of our new neighbors? Did I want to seem brusque, uncooperative and stand-offish? Lilias and I debated the pros and cons and reached a painful and fateful decision. I accepted.

As the day approached I tried to soothe my apprehensions with consoling thoughts. I liked books and was always talking about them anyway. Maybe delivering a lecture on books wouldn't be so very different. I would be talking to strangers instead of to a few friends. I would be talking standing up instead of sitting down. And no one could interrupt. And I planned to discuss books which I had recently read and reviewed and so, presumably, I would know more about them than any of the ladies in the audience, a consideration which also ought to bolster my self-confidence. Nevertheless, when the day came I wondered why I had ever been foolish enough to let myself become trapped in so dismaying an occasion. As we drove to the lecture Lilias tried to encourage me by being bright and cheerful, but her efforts were labored and her smile seemed forced. My hands were perspiring.

About fifty women were seated on little gilt chairs in the living room and hall of a handsome brick house. When I rose to speak I found it absolutely necessary to clutch the back of my chair with a frantic grip. I had to hunch over awkwardly to reach it, but I dared not let go. Nevertheless, as I got under way my taut nerves began to uncoil. Words were coming in a steady flow and, what was even more encouraging, they were actually arranging themselves into well-constructed sentences. The ladies seemed interested. They even laughed when I hoped they would. Without realizing how it had happened I found that I had let go of the chair top, that I was standing upright, that I was blessedly relaxed and—oh, wonder of wonders!—that I was enjoying myself. When the lecture was over, many of the ladies said kind things and I left flushed with triumph. Lecturing? Why, there was nothing to it! Anyone who knew anything about his subject could lecture.

A few days later I lunched in New York with a friend who was the publicity director of a well-known publishing house. As an example of the perils of moving to Connecticut I told him about my only lecture experience. "Would you like to lecture professionally?" he asked. The idea had never occurred to me. "If you would," he went on, "I know a girl who is the publicity director at the Colston Leigh Bureau. They're always looking for new speakers. Would you like me to tell her about you?"

Would I? I didn't know. Still—I had to read the books anyway. It would be nice to earn more money. It would be gratifying to prove to myself that I could do something which I had never even dreamed of doing until that moment. On the other hand—"I don't know what to say," I replied. "You're very kind. If Colston Leigh should be interested I don't suppose it could do any harm to talk to him. But I'm not at all sure that I want to lecture."

A few days later I received a telephone call from Mr. Leigh's office. Would I come to see him? I would. I did. Bob had told me that Colston Leigh was the aggressive and tremendously successful head of the largest agency in the lecture business. But he had not mentioned, if he knew, that Mr. Leigh's private office was one of the largest in any business. As I walked from the door toward his huge desk in a distant corner, it took me so long to get there that I felt a little like an Italian underling summoned into the august presence of Mussolini. "So you want to be a lecturer," said Mr. Leigh.

I felt an oddly unexpected thrill of satisfaction. I wasn't at all sure that I wanted to be a lecturer. I had allowed Bob to drop a hint in the right quarter, but I was seated there in Mr. Leigh's office more out of curiosity than anything else. After all, he had asked me to come. I had not applied for an interview. "No," I said. "I don't think I want to be a lecturer, at least not right now. But I gave a lecture recently, which was successful, and I might be interested if I knew more about it. I was curious enough to come to see you when you asked me to."

Mr. Leigh looked shocked and surprised. Probably he didn't have to persuade most potential lecturers. But he recovered his habitual aplomb at once and launched into an exposition of the lecture business, methods of booking, agency commissions (enormous), standards of conduct expected of his clients (lecturers are not supposed to drink to excess or to make passes at lady program chairmen), and the vast sums earned by successful speakers. He showed no interest whatever in hearing me speak or in having someone from his office hear me and report on my ability. Evidently my word that my maiden effort had gone well was enough.

The longer Colston Leigh talked, the more intrigued I became. I had not been able to find another job during the great Calhoun crisis. Now here was another profession, an alternative or supplementary line of work, being thrust upon me without any effort on my part. I signed up. That was in the autumn of 1939. I made my first professional lecture in January, 1940. And I continued to lecture for more than fourteen years, "retiring from the platform" in the pompous phrase of the lecture business, in February, 1954.

Dozens of books and hundreds of articles have been

written about the trials and tribulations of the lecture circuit in America. Some have been light-hearted and humorous; many have been sarcastic and venomous. It is always easy to bite the hand which feeds you, always tempting to the unpleasant underside of human nature to sneer in a superior manner at persons poorly informed about one's specialty.

But artistic and literary intellectuals, who specialize in Greek drama, Chinese porcelain or Byzantine architecture, are able to do so only because other people, the laborers, farmers and businessmen who keep our economic system working, create enough surplus capital so that funds are available for non-utilitarian purposes. It is that extra money which educates and trains specialists and which pays them for lecturing on the arts. Theoretically, it would be nice if everybody cared deeply about one or several arts; but those who do care have an obligation, it seems to me, to be grateful to those who care only on alternate Tuesdays, or do not care at all. For, it is these "Philistines" who by their daily labors make it possible for an ever-growing minority to participate in and to patronize the arts—make it possible for thousands of organizations to hire thousands of specialists to lecture on hundreds of subjects.

The men and women who make all this possible are usually specialists, too, in other important subjects, such as manufacturing and selling, cooking and baby care, about which the specialists are woefully ignorant. It is a cheap and petty form of condescension for lecturers to make fun of the people who pay them to lecture. Nevertheless, strange adventures do befall lecturers and lecture audiences do vary enormously.

There was the time in my first season of lecturing

when I walked into a shabby old hotel in a small Pennsylvania city where I was scheduled to address a businessmen's luncheon. It was my first encounter with such a typically American function. Sounds of revelry were coming from the bar. I entered and found my prospective audience lined up two or three deep, drinking two or three martinis apiece, a procedure which I learned later is not customary with most local chapters of their national organization.

The members were wearing those cardboard placards the size and shape of butter plates with "Call me Jake" or "Call me Al" or "Hank" or "Dutch" printed on them. I was a little late; so the chairman pounced upon me, broke up the gathering without offering me a chance to fortify myself as everyone else had done so carefully, and swept us all into the dreary, crowded dining room. There members relaxed, throwing the hard rolls at each other and flipping butter pats like schoolboys. By the time they had sung "Happy Birthday to You" to the three members who had birthdays during the week, the atmosphere had become so literary that my feet were cold with alarm. What on earth was I doing there?

Finally the chairman rose and rapped for order. "It gives me great pleasure," he shouted, leaning perilously over his ice cream, "to see so many of you here today. But I am afraid I know the reason why. Two weeks ago I announced that we would have Miss America with us today, and that she would model the newest line of Jantzen bathing suit. Unfortunately, the Rotarians, whose budget is in a much more satisfactory condition than our own, have outbid us. But Mr. Prescott will speak on literature instead."

There was the time I was engaged to speak to a large

but exclusive organization of the most highly educated and socially prominent young women in a great city. Among several distinguished guests assembled for the occasion was Sigrid Undset, Norwegian Nobel Prize winner, world-famous author of *Kristan Lavransdatter*. On either side of the great writer at the speakers' table sat two of the smartest, most attractive members of the club. On either side of them sat my wife and I. The place cards were illegible. The young woman between me and Mme. Undset nudged me, gestured toward the massive and formidably silent celebrity and whispered, "Who is she?"

"Undset, Nobel Prize," I wrote on the back of my place card. Only a blank stare. "Sigrid," I added. "Norwegian." Still no look of intelligent comprehension troubled her pretty but bewildered face. "Author of *Kristin Lavransdatter*," I scribbled furiously. "What's the matter? Can't you read my handwriting?" "Yes," wrote my charming hostess, "but I never heard of her."

Later Lilias told me a similar story. On her side of the monumental author, ignorance was even more sublime. There couldn't be such a thing as a Norwegian writer, because everybody knows that Norwegians speak Swedish.

There was the time I went to a manufacturing town in New Jersey to speak in the local library. About an hour before the lecture was scheduled to begin, a rainstorm of nearly hurricane force broke over the town. The rains descended and the floods blocked some of the streets and swept over the sidewalks in many places. The gale flung water on the library windows as if a fire hose were being played upon them. When the head librarian ushered me into the main reading room, where chairs for some one hundred and fifty persons were arranged in neat rows, seven people were sitting in the audience. Not one of

them sat in the same row as anyone else, or anywhere near anyone else. And alone in the middle of the front row sat a gaunt and haggard individual who looked so much like Boris Karloff in his Frankenstein's monster make-up, I thought I must be the victim of someone's gruesome idea of a practical joke.

I began to speak, trying to be informal, trying to relax the tense atmosphere by some remarks to the effect that even a lecture on fiction was preferable to being out in the storm. The other six characters smiled politely. The monster's expression did not change. During the hour-long lecture the monster never moved and never changed his grim, blank stare. It was unnerving. He didn't look interested. He didn't look bored. He hardly looked alive. He hardly looked human. When the lecture was over he stalked with a robot's slow, mechanical shuffle out of the room, his hands hanging nearer to his knees than any hands I have ever seen before or since.

"Who is that frightful creature?" I asked the librarian. She didn't know. She had never seen him before. And she devoutly hoped that she would never see him again, particularly on a dark street on a rainy night, a hope I shared.

There was the time in another New Jersey library that a wildly excited man rose from his seat in the middle of the lecture and denounced me in terms of violent abuse, but so vaguely that I could not understand what I had done to provoke him. After several minutes of complete confusion and general consternation bordering on panic, he subsided as suddenly as he had erupted and I resumed speaking.

As soon as the lecture was finished the librarian rushed up to me, overflowing with apologies. "I'm so sorry," she said. "I just knew that something dreadful would happen as soon as I noticed him in the audience. You mustn't mind what he said, Mr. Prescott. He's done this sort of thing before. You see, he isn't really crazy. At least, they don't keep him locked up permanently. He just got back from the asylum again last week. He'll probably have to go back in a few weeks or a few months at the most. He's always had to before."

There was the time, the only one in fourteen years, when I completely forgot an engagement. I was supposed to be speaking at a women's club on Long Island and only learned of my crime when my agent telephoned me twenty minutes after the lecture was scheduled to begin. And the time I addressed a dinner club of men and women in a small Massachusetts city and was introduced by a mournful gentleman who announced that this was the last meeting of the club because the members did not seem to care about hearing lectures and the whole idea had been well intentioned, but a mistake, a costly mistake. And the time during the Second World War that I made an appointment to donate blood on the morning of the same day I was booked to speak to the Women's Club of Garden City in the early afternoon. I gave the blood, fainted dead away and took a long time to recover sufficiently so that I could totter from the Red Cross station. I gave the lecture, too, in spite of the fact that I was in a cold sweat the whole time, clutching the lectern to keep from falling while the room spun in circles, twice nearly fainting again.

After two years with the Colston Leigh Bureau I decided that I might be able to do better for myself, both in number of engagements and fees, in a smaller organization whose "attractions" did not include quite so many world-famous celebrities or quite so many literary critics. I transferred to the Harold Peat Agency and remained there for eight years. The fact that I became a daily book critic on *The New York Times* shortly after I made the change was a substantial boost to my lecture career.

It meant that no longer could I tour for several weeks at a time. I was tied down to my deadlines for copy. But it also meant that my name carried more weight, that more organizations would hire me and would pay more—not much compared with the fat fees obtained by the great stars of the lecture circuit, but more than before. In 1950 I transferred again and spent my last four years as a lecturer with the Lee Keedick Bureau. My relations with all three concerns were serene and pleasant and I am grateful to the kind and helpful people in all of them.

Ever since hundreds of thousands of Americans battled for tickets to hear Dickens and Thackeray, Mark Twain and Artemus Ward, the lecture business in the United States has been a subject of controversy and a source of myths and legends. Born in the nineteenth century, fostered by a commendable desire for self-improvement and for contact with something vague called culture, it has survived the demise of its greatest single support, the Chautauqua circuit. And although it has suffered a moderate recession during the last few years, it has managed to survive the mortal competition of the movies, the radio and television. Those media of mass entertainment may reach millions of persons daily. But also daily from September to June, scores of thousands of persons assemble in handsome auditoriums and in dreary basement playrooms to listen to speakers bringing them facts and opinions on Japanese flower arrangement, life among the

Trobriand Islanders, the nature of the world crisis, and the nature of Dylan Thomas' and T. S. Eliot's poetry.

Why do so many people like to listen to lectures? I often asked myself while I listened to the minutes of the last meeting, the announcements of the elections of new members and the singing of club songs and the national anthem. And after years of speculation I concluded that there is one major reason and many minor ones. The major reason is that men and women are social animals and like to gather in groups. Such gathering has to have a purpose. The nominal purpose in attending lectures is exposure to culture. The most influential, minor, often unformulated purpose is to be entertained.

A competent lecturer, no matter how serious or even abstruse his subject, always makes certain that he entertains his audience. If he does not, if he only instructs his listeners, he will not remain long in the lecture business. Part of his ability to entertain lies in his sincerity, his belief in the importance of his subject and his skill in making it interesting. An equally important element in his ability to entertain lies in his projection of personality, his skill in amusing his listeners, in winning their respect for his knowledge and their liking for him personally.

In other words, every successful lecturer is a showman as well as a specialist. If he did not have an element of the ham actor in him, if his egoism did not respond to the opportunity to stand on a brightly lit platform and address others, he probably never would have become a lecturer in the first place.

But most people who attend a lecture don't want to be entertained only; they insist on being persuaded that they have spent their time profitably, that their experience has been rewarding in terms of new ideas, new facts and new insights. Consequently, if a speaker is too entertaining and does not provide sufficiently solid cultural fare he will irritate his listeners, who always resent being talked down to. A certain amount of instruction is essential to justify the lecture at all and to avoid bruising the self-respect of the members of the audience. So the lecturer must steer a careful course between the Scylla of too much entertainment and disastrous condescension and the Charybdis of too much instruction and fatal boredom.

Although entertainment and instruction are the only important commodities a lecturer has to sell, some of the people who come to hear him are not much interested in either. They are lured to the lecture by curiosity, a desire to see in the flesh a celebrity of whom they have long heard, or an alleged celebrity of whom they have never heard before. The celebrity may be world-famous, a senator, an explorer, the author of an international best seller; or he may have won only a small reputation in the narrow world of his specialty. The curious, naturally enough, will pay more and come in larger numbers to hear Eleanor Roosevelt or Jawaharlal Nehru than they will to hear less famous and distinguished people who have become authorities in their special fields. But some of them will come to hear the minor figures. They want to know what he is like, this curious person who has made a career of bees or books.

Another motive considerably stronger than idle curiosity is purely social: the human craving to belong, to acquire status by membership in an organization not open to the general public. If you wish to enjoy the pleasure and prestige of membership in the Women's Civic Club or the Advertising Men's Thursday Luncheon Club, you must listen politely to the regular speakers. They are traditional and cannot be dodged.

Somewhat different circumstances account for the attendance at lectures in schools and colleges. There are the captive audiences who have no choice. The lecture is compulsory. There are the student intellectuals genuinely interested in the speaker and his subject. And there are the normal young, bored with the monotony of education and its too familiar routine, who are willing to try anything once if it promises to be a change.

In these United States today there are about twenty-five major bureaus and agencies whose principal business is the booking of lectures. In addition, there are several hundred small ones. Some of the lecture agencies also book musicians, singers and dancers. There are approximately 2,500 professional organizations, schools and colleges which engage lecturers through professional bureaus.

These figures are staggering. But they do not give a precise picture of all the lecturing which goes on in the country. In one respect they are too large, in another too small. They are too large because many professional lecturers speak infrequently, either because they are too busy to find the time or because they are not very successful. And many organizations which engage speakers have such small budgets that they hire only one or two professional lecturers a year. They eke out their other programs with amateurs. It is these amateurs who make our figures too small. No one knows how many people speak without payment, for the publicity, for the gratification of their vanity, or for the opportunity to promote the good causes which they cherish. Their numbers are unknown, but their name is legion.

How valuable is a series of lectures sponsored by a community organization? There is no way of telling. The value, of course, depends on the quality of the lecturers and of the audiences. A few professional lecturers are brilliant. Many are exceedingly able. Others are glib, superficial, pretentious and inane. Some of these are distressingly popular—men who spout sentimental balderdash about how to be happy, successful, admired by the opposite sex and at peace with the infinite; women who "review" books, which means that they itemize one novel's plot for a full hour, acting out its crucial scenes to the best of their inadequate abilities as monologue artists, utterly falsifying the author's work and destroying forever any inclination in their listeners to read the book in question.

The quality of lecture audiences varies enormously, but on the whole it is considerably higher than one might suspect from reading the sarcastic explosions of temper let loose by some disgruntled speakers. Every audience contains both alert and intelligent people and stupid and mentally lazy people. Believing as I do that most lecturers are sincere in their beliefs and at least competent as speakers, and that most members of their audiences are of average or superior intelligence and pay their speakers respectful attention, I am convinced that the American lecture circuit contributes usefully to the cause of general culture and adult education.

When hundreds of able men and women speak to thousands of attentive and intelligent people, the ideas they champion must strike a spark in many minds. If the lecturer is also a writer, his listeners would do better to read his books than to listen to him talk. But everyone is not a reader of books. It is better to listen to a condensed version of an idea than not to encounter it at all. Those members of the audience who are blissfully indifferent to everything the speaker says suffer no permanent harm from an hour spent in the soothing pastime of ignoring a lecturer. And those who do care, who sit up and pay strict attention, may acquire a new understanding of some aspect of the arts or of politics for which they will long be grateful.

Looking at the upturned faces beneath him, a lecturer is tempted to think that he can tell what lies behind them, that he can distinguish the intelligent from the stupid, the fascinated from the bored. But he can't. All he can tell is that some faces register alert attention and that some register nothing at all. The animated face may reflect only its owner's pleasure in being away from her kitchen and her children for a refreshing interval, or her appreciation of a pleasantry; and the noncommittal face may wear the natural expression of a thoughtful person joyfully clutching at the speaker's most cherished ideas.

In the movies the passage of time and the multiplication of experience are often suggested by glimpses of fluttering calendar leaves, of turning railroad wheels, of faces in a crowd, of sunrises and sunsets. My memories of lecturing sometimes seem similar. They include reading books and writing columns about them in day coaches, parlor cars and Pullmans, in railroad and bus stations, in bleak hotel rooms and in chintzy guest rooms in the program chairmen's homes. They include boarding trains at one o'clock in the morning and getting off trains at six in the morning, riding in buses and airplanes and in the private cars of kind strangers who took much time and trouble to help a wandering lecturer upon his way. They include reception committees, interviews by reporters from local newspapers and from school and college publications, chicken-patty-and-green-pea luncheons, formal dinners (black tie) and informal receptions (coffee and dough-nuts and nothing more stimulating for a weary per-former). They include many kind, attractive and charm-ing people, and, of course, some dull, depressing, peculiar people.

In my fourteen years of lecturing I spoke in every state east of the Mississippi and north of the Mason-Dixon line save Maine and Vermont, and in four states below the line, Maryland, Virginia, West Virginia and Kentucky. I spoke in big cities and in country villages, at nine in the morning and at ten at night, in gigantic auditoriums and in the living rooms of small apartments, in country clubs, department stores, restaurants, theatres, libraries, hotel ballrooms, college chapels and school gymnasiums. I ad-dressed forums, town halls, businessmen's luncheons, resort hotel guests, classes in writing, students of all ages, professional societies of English teachers, university pro-fessors and librarians, and women's clubs—most often, women's clubs.

There were two good reasons for my concentration on women's clubs. The first is that they comprise by far the largest segment of the lecture circuit, and the law of averages made them my most important customers. The second is that most women's clubs make a point of includ-ing at least one book or literary lecture every season, while other organizations prefer topical discussions, travel talks or whatever. Most new books sold and read in the United States are sold to women and read by them. This is not true of many kinds of books (sport, adventure, war, etc.) and may not be true of any particular book. But it is es-pecially true of fiction.

Somehow, in spite of the demands made upon their time and energy by children, housework and community affairs, women do find more time for reading than most men. And when women don't read because they don't care a bit about reading, they usually think it necessary to make a polite pretense that they read and care. This accounts for the necessity women's club program chairmen feel to engage a lecturer to talk on books. And it makes the atmosphere wonderfully warm and cozy for the literary lecturer.

The opposite is true of men's organizations, particularly of businessmen's lunch clubs, which are the most difficult of all audiences for a literary critic to address. Most of the members do not read books, see no reason why they should and seem to enjoy defying the speaker on books to interest them. What is worse, they seem innately suspicious of literature and frankly hostile to a professional critic, who must, they seem to think, be somewhat effeminate if he makes his living out of such a feminine pursuit as reading and writing. These remarks, of course, do not apply to all men's luncheon groups and certainly not to all which I addressed. But they apply to enough so that a literary critic's engagement to speak at the downtown lunch club of any American city probably means that the club is unusually broad-minded and tolerant, or that the critic is unusually sure of himself, or that he needs the job and is willing to face the risks.

Women's clubs vary from town to town and within the same town. Some are old, conservative and exclusive. Some are new, bustling and folksy. There are pretty and smart women in most of them, and plain and dowdy women in most of them, too. I never spoke at any women's club in which I did not notice a number of extremely attractive women. Nor did I ever speak to one whose members did not include one or two ladies who could have posed for one of Helen Hokinson's good-naturedly satirical cartoons.

And I found that women's clubs, like chicken yards, have their pecking order. Certain ladies dominate other ladies whether they are officers of the club or not. One usually rules the roost. If she is typical she is considerably wealthier than most of her fellow members and she enjoys a more exalted social position. Accustomed to deference, an enthusiastic lion hunter, she assumes that it is her prerogative to entertain visiting celebrities. Often she is gracious, charming and thoughtfully hospitable; sometimes she is vain, stuffy and arrogant. In any case it is she who gives the little luncheon or dinner party before the lecture (that is, if the club is not feeding the speaker officially), who asks a few choice spirits in to meet the tired lecturer after he has earned his fee. She often has signed photographs of the more eminent lecturers on her living room table and may casually refer to John Mason Brown as Jack, or to Edward Weeks as Ted.

I have many pleasant memories of charming women whose kindness and consideration did much to brighten the tedium of busy lecture trips. But I have some surprising memories, too. Two of them I think should be recorded here.

Once I had an engagement to speak in a Middle Western city and my train was scheduled to arrive at seven o'clock in the morning. Several weeks in advance the local social leader wrote me a letter inviting me to breakfast. "Come right out as soon as your train gets in." With some trepidation I accepted. It might be pleasanter and would certainly be cheaper to read and write before my three o'clock lecture in the lady's library rather than in an hotel room. But to walk in for breakfast at seven-thirty seemed

Vasiliu

embarrassingly early. After all, I was a stranger in those parts. So I sat for an hour in the station waiting room and then took a taxi which deposited me upon her doorstep at quarter past eight, surely, I thought, an early enough hour in which to call upon an unknown lady.

The door was opened by a man wearing his hat and coat and carrying a briefcase. "Mr. Prescott?" he said. "I'm Mr. So-and-So. I'm sorry I can't stay, but some of us have work to do, you know, ha! ha! ha! We can't sit around all day chatting with the ladies. My wife will be right down. Good-bye."

I laid my coat, hat, typewriter and bundle of books on a bench in the front hall and sat down in the living room. Sounds and smells of cooking came from the kitchen through the swinging dining room door. In a few minutes Mrs. So-and-So did come down, or, rather, she made an entrance.

She was dressed in orange and black lounging pajamas with a leopard skin pattern, sandals which did not hide her bare feet and purple toenail polish, and a long black stole. Her facial make-up was elaborate and conspicuous and gleamed like cheaply glazed china. It had obviously taken a good half-hour's careful application. "Chawmed to see you, Mr. Prescott," she murmured hoarsely in a voice reminiscent of Jeanne Eagels playing Sadie Thompson. "Shawl we breakfawst?"

Another occasion which surprised me equally might even have some significance in the mysterious realm of feminine psychology. It was a few months after the publication of Kathleen Winsor's *Forever Amber*, that sensational best-selling romance about lust and lechery at the court of Charles II. I was making a brief tour among the small cities of upstate New York, speaking at five different women's clubs in as many days. Since Miss Winsor's novel was the most widely read book in the United States at that time, I discussed it at each lecture and each time rendered a severely unfavorable verdict.

And after each lecture the same woman, it almost seemed, came up to speak to me. Of course, it wasn't the same woman, but she always seemed to be wearing the same hat, one alarmingly similar to those beloved by the late dowager Queen Mary of England.

"Mr. Prescott," she would say. "I'm the wife of the Methodist clergyman here and I want to tell you how delighted I was to hear what you said about *Forever Amber*. I agree with you completely."

"I'm glad that you agree with me," I would reply. "But I am a little surprised that you read a book like *Forever Amber*."

"Oh, yes, I read it," lips pursed with disapproval.

"Did you read it all?"

"Oh, yes, I read it all."

"Well, I hope you won't mind my asking, but if you disapprove of it so strongly, why did you read it all?"

"Because I wanted to see if it was that bad all the way through and it was."

This may be considered as important evidence of the fascination which the bad women of the world, in this case Amber St. Clair, have always had for the good women of the world since the times of Helen of Troy and Cleopatra.

· fourteen ·

One afternoon in March, 1942, as I sat in my library reading a book for my weekly column in *Cue*, the telephone rang and Lilias interrupted my labors to say that New York was calling me. With no more than my usual idle curiosity I answered the phone. "Just a minute," said a secretarial voice and I was connected with the managing editor of *The New York Times*. Would I be interested in writing book reviews for the daily book page of the *Times*? Could I come in to his office to talk about it on the following day? Needless to say, I could and would, although I tried not to sound too eager while saying so. As soon as I hung up I shouted the glad tidings to Lilias, and our joy and excitement were so explosive that Peter, then aged six, was quite confounded. With considerable apprehension he asked "Is it good or bad?"

My interview with that great newspaperman, the late Edwin L. James, went smoothly enough, but it caused me more inner tension than it need have. At that time I knew that Mr. James was eminent in his profession, but I knew nothing else about him. It was not until after I had been with the *Times* for some time that I discovered that his gruff bark and blunt manner were only devices to speed interviews and to save time. Mr. James would never bother with civilities about the weather. Chewing his cigar in silence he would wait with restrained impatience for you to state your business. If it was reasonable, his kind and thoughtful consideration could be counted on. At my first interview I was engaged to write three columns a week, with the understanding that my employment was provisional for three months but that I could consider my job permanent if I was still with the *Times* after that period. A year and a half later, in September, 1944, my stint was increased to four columns a week, the number which I have written continuously since then.

To be a daily book critic on the greatest newspaper in the United States was more than I had dared hope for. Although I had knocked on the door of *The New York Times Book Review,* it had not been opened to me. I had contributed reviews to several literary media, but they had been discouragingly few. Up to that moment I had felt adequately stimulated by my job of writing the book column for a weekly New York magazine. And now by a series of fortunate chances, which included a sudden opening on the *Times* and the fact that a *Cue* reader who liked my work had mentioned it to a *Times* executive just as the vacancy occurred, opportunity was making its celebrated single knock.

My resignation from *Cue* was only technical, for I continued as a contributor and wrote *Cue's* book column for another five years. But the change in my life and work was enormous. My *Cue* reviews were brief, almost telegraphic in style, concise descriptions and flat verdicts. My *Times* reviews averaged 900 words. This left room for maneuver, room for more detailed information, for critical discussion, for serious efforts to suggest the characteristic quality and atmosphere of a book, and for such personal flourishes as seemed in keeping with the *Times'* generally dignified demeanor. In other words, I would not only render judgments to the best of my ability, as I did at *Cue*, I would also write to the best of my ability, which had been impossible in the cramped confines of my short *Cue* column.

For several thousand years critics have been debating the nature and function of literary criticism without reaching agreement. Small wonder then that popular misconceptions and curious legends abound. Many mistaken ideas about criticism would be eliminated, it seems to me, if one basic truth were more generally understood. This is that all criticism consists of only two things: information and highly personal opinion.

There can be no dispute about the information: the author is so-and-so who has written a novel about such-and-such from the point of view of a ten-year-old idiot child in a soupy prose clogged with odd words and curious incidents which may or may not have symbolical significance. The opinion comes in when the critic expresses his own ideas as to the success of the author in his project; on whether the project was worth undertaking in the first place; on what view of the lot of man the author is dramatizing in his work; and on whether those verbal difficulties are really symbols and what they symbolize if they are.

Critics differ from each other on what information they think it important to provide, in the more or less predictable nature of their reactions to certain types of writing, and in their personalities as reflected in their writing. Much of the difference between critics is explained by the differences in their individual characters shaped by their experience of life and of books; part of the difference is caused by the critics' conception of the readers who will encounter their reviews.

A review destined to appear in a magazine for teen-age girls is necessarily somewhat different from one intended for the dignified pages of *The American Scholar,* although both could conceivably be written by the same person. "A mere reviewer" (an epithet nearly always used with derogatory intent) writes in a noticeably different manner from a journalistic critic. An academic critic in his turn usually writes according to the customs of his tribe, which are not those of journalistic critics. Sometimes, of course, when an academic critic contributes to a popular publication he feels it necessary to unbend a trifle in the hope of being understood. Let us be more precise about these classifications.

"'A mere reviewer" writes for newspapers or magazines and is content to treat books as news. He announces their publication, identifies their authors, briefly describes their contents and sometimes, but not always, renders a verdict. If he is an incompetent "mere reviewer," he may even summarize a novel's plot, which is the unforgivable sin of reviewing.

"Mere reviews" are highly useful to prospective readers and do not deserve the scornful disparagement with which literary intellectuals often dismiss them. Every journalistic critic in his never-ending battle with masses of print and his perpetual struggle to meet a succession of deadlines for copy sometimes writes "mere reviews."

But journalistic critics, who also write for newspapers and general magazines, try whenever possible to climb out of the valley of "mere reviewing" onto the plateau of genuine criticism. This means that they perform every service the "mere reviewer" does, but in addition try to do much more. They try by their own skill with words to suggest the unique quality which distinguishes one book from all other books; to indicate the nature of its technical construction; to identify the outlook on life expressed and, if that outlook seems particularly misguided, to say so; to judge the book in question in comparison with other books of its kind; and in the process of all this to write a brief essay which will be interesting and worth reading whether the book discussed is worth reading or not. No wonder, then, that journalistic critics age before their time, develop harried expressions, nervous tics and duodenal ulcers, and become violently allergic to particular authors.

Both "mere reviewers" and journalistic critics write for educated readers who care enough about books to read reviews, but who are not literary scholars or high-caste intellectuals.

The academic critics contribute to popular publications when the chance offers, but most of their work appears in learned journals and in book form. They are usually professors and usually they write for other professors, for serious students and for literary intellectuals. They are delighted to discuss current books if they are by currently fashionable writers (Faulkner, Hemingway, Henry Green, Graham Greene, Sartre and Camus); but more frequently they write about established if not classic writers who, they believe, need reinterpretation (James, Melville, Hawthorne); or about writers not too long dead who, they believe, need rediscovery (Ford Madox Ford, Scott Fitzgerald, Stephen Crane).

Academic critics writing for a select circle of initiates concentrate, quite properly, on professional aspects of the books under consideration: on highly technical analyses of structure, vocabulary, philosophy, and possible symbolical meaning. They speculate darkly about the author's id and libido. Sometimes such involved criticism is brilliant. Usually it is learned. And often it is dull and nearly unintelligible—this last because of the pseudo-scientific vocabulary and pedantic jargon to which a number of the ablest academic critics are addicted.

Why men who devote great abilities and a lifetime of study to literature and presumably care passionately about the art of writing should write so wretchedly themselves is a baffling mystery. But many an intellectually formidable feat of literary analysis is written in a vile and tortuous prose which is almost in itself evidence of its author's lack of any feeling for the chaste beauties of the English language.

The academic critics may not be widely read, but they are enormously influential because they are intensively read in colleges and universities by the professors and instructors who help to form the minds of the young people who in their turn will be professors, instructors and writers.

During the last decade the influence of some of the most brilliant and respected academic critics has been responsible for a fashion in modern fiction which exalts symbolism above all other literary techniques. Consequently, lesser critics frequently jump onto the bandwagon with loud cries that they have found and interpreted the symbols in the works of some innocent bystander of an author who, if he were alive, would not recognize a symbol if it were served up to him for breakfast. Another result of the present vogue for symbolism is that some young writers feel it essential to write pretentious and obscure allegories. If they did not, who knows but that they might be excommunicated and sentenced to permanent exile far from the groves of academe and the select company of the happy few.

Like all critical fashions carried to excess, the cult of symbolism is certain to pass away in due season. For the present it may be regarded as a fine demonstration of the power of an idea when it is defended by highly articulate and exceedingly solemn champions.

Reviews of new books in the United States are published in four principal varieties of media: those which specialize in reviewing new books, such as *The Saturday Review* and the Sunday book supplements of *The New York Times, The New York Herald Tribune* and *The Chicago Tribune;* daily newspapers with weekly departments devoted to books or with daily book columns; magazines with regular departments devoted to book reviews, of which the most influential are *The New Yorker, Time, Newsweek, Harper's* and *The Atlantic Monthly;* and magazines edited for special and limited groups, the scholarly and learned journals.

The reviews published in the book supplements are usually written by outside contributors. These are the men and women who in the editor's opinion have special qualifications to discuss particular books. Thus many writers of established reputation occasionally contribute reviews. Some novelists review regularly and are almost as well known as critics as they are as the authors of their own books. War correspondents review books about war; foreign correspondents, books about the countries they have covered; anthropologists, books about anthropology; and professors of eighteenth-century English literature, books about Boswell and Johnson.

The theory is that only experts can speak with authority. But in practice it sometimes means that professional rivals review each other's books with glacial scorn, or that members of the same small club review each other's books with extravagant enthusiasm. Most such authoritative experts write excellent journalistic criticism. But there are a few of such Olympian pretensions that they refuse to modify their customary professional jargon for the benefit of the readers of Sunday newspapers, who are left to shift for themselves and make what they can out of the viscid prose and weird vocabulary of the ultra academic critics.

The regular book review departments of magazines and newspapers are usually written by staff members who are specialists in books in general, but who are not authorities on anything in particular. They are, presumably, well educated and widely read, enthusiastic but discriminating lovers of books. Being human, they have their noticeable literary and even political prejudices. They disagree with each other regularly, criticism being the personal, emotional and opinionated business that it is. They make mistakes, overpraising here, undervaluing there. But their very shortcomings and crotchets help to guide their readers, who become familiar with them and adjust accordingly.

And just because they are not authorities, their descriptions and opinions of new books may be more helpful to prospective readers than those of a specialist who has devoted his life to the subject. The journalistic critic may not be able to tell whether a new history of the War of the Spanish Succession is presenting an entirely new theory about the foreign policy of Louis XIV, but he can tell his readers whether he thinks the book is interesting and well written and what its general thesis is. And maybe that is what they want most to know.

The journalistic critic who practices his profession for a considerable time inevitably swallows an immense amount of miscellaneous information. Of this he can remember only a little, a smattering of many subjects and perhaps a more substantial amount about those which appeal to him personally. And when these subjects pop up again in a newer book still, as they invariably do, he can even write with an appearance of learning which those who know less than he find exceedingly impressive.

Every year approximately 10,000 new books are published in the United States. Of these about half are school and college textbooks, books on law, medicine, theology, electrical engineering, baby care and other technical subjects unsuitable for review in a daily newspaper. The rest, the so-called "trade books" (meaning the book shop trade), are the books of fiction, biography, history, travel, poetry, current affairs and a dozen varieties of miscellaneous which compete for review space.

No one who has not cowered in alarm as the flood of such books pours across his desk has any conception of its dismaying volume. Publishers have a vague idea because they have seen the statistics. But they have no really clear notion, because they are too close to the titles on their own lists to realize how many their competitors are bringing out.

Publishers are often too close to their "big book" of the moment to realize how many other books are scheduled for publication at the same time, many of them also "big books." This is understandable, for they have spent many hours and much thought soothing its author's ruffled feelings. They have patiently and tactfully persuaded him to cut here and rewrite there. They have argued with the artist, who is supposed to produce a jacket picture which is both legitimately decorative and alluring to potential purchasers. They have delivered pep talks to their salesmen and debated to the last penny how much advertising is justified. And all this effort may be devoted to a novel which is professionally competent but without distinction of any kind, or to a lush hash of historical nonsense called *Memphis Mamie*.

During the week of its publication, however, there may also be published two books by deservedly famous writers, six by promising newcomers, a dozen on important topical subjects, and six other hack historical romances. Consequently *Memphis Mamie* is reviewed briefly with a batch of other new novels in the back pages of the book supplements and isn't mentioned at all in magazine and daily newspaper book departments. Its author, his wife and his mother-in-law may write letters calling *Memphis Mamie* to the attention of reviewers. They may telephone them. They may even drop in on them at their offices. The only result of such desperate measures is mutual embarrassment. With space at a premium nothing can be done for such a book.

New books pour in in such a formidable torrent, often more than fifty a day, that much of any critic's time must be spent in just sorting them out. In the "Books of The Times" office we divide them as they arrive: those which we will list and briefly identify on their publication day in a column called "Books Published Today," and those which we won't mention at all. This is necessary because we do not have enough space to list all books and because the listing is selective, the exercise of an editorial function.

We don't list textbooks and technical books, scholarly

books obviously intended for a professional body of readers, books written in foreign languages, books privately printed or printed in mimeograph form. This policy of deciding for ourselves which books to include in our listing has vastly annoyed several publishers who refuse to grant to the *Times* the right to conduct its columns as it sees fit. A recent example of such questionable indignation was a bitter protest made by the publisher of a book which described in minute detail the various practices of sexual perversion. We did not budge in our contention that his book was suitable only for the medical profession. He furiously insisted that it was written for the general public. If it was, a more cynical commercial venture in publishing could hardly be imagined.

The books which we decide should be listed are then divided into those which might possibly be reviewed and those which, though worthy of listing, seem to be of insufficient general interest or of insufficient literary respectability to make them candidates for review. The two groups merge and overlap, and include books on special subjects—such as pottery, cookery, interior decoration, how-to-do-it books, inspirational self-help books, religious books, Westerns, most detective stories and most science fiction, "drug-store rental library fiction" and nearly all publications of vanity houses (firms which publish books at their authors' expense instead of their own). The reviewable books are then arranged on our shelves in chronological order according to their publication dates.

Which, then, of these theoretically reviewable books are reviewed? Only a few, of course, for the "Books of The Times" column appears six days a week, 312 times a year, and usually is devoted to only one book. At such a rate we can only scratch the surface of competent and reviewable books. But my colleague on the *Times* book page, Charles Poore, and I hope that we do not neglect many important books. We know that we have to pass by many books which are important to their authors, which were produced in agonizing anxiety with laborious toil, and many which are important to particular groups of readers—bird watchers, old button collectors, theosophists, members of this and that. But if we decide not to review a particular book and our colleagues on other publications express enough enthusiasm to persuade us that we made a mistake, we can always pick it up and review it a little late. This happens several times every year.

The problem of selection is painful, a matter of anxious and much time-consuming indecision. For my own guidance I have developed a three-point system. The first is news value. After all, I am writing for a newspaper and many books are news in themselves, books by Winston Churchill, Dwight D. Eisenhower, Harry S. Truman, Jawaharlal Nehru, Chiang Kai-shek, statesmen, soldiers, scientists, explorers, mountain climbers, and celebrities from many disparate walks of life.

Books often have news value not because of their authors' fame and importance but because of the importance of their subjects, such as the current state of affairs in Washington, London, Paris, Moscow, New Delhi, Johannesburg; such as war, peace, the United Nations, atomic energy, population and natural resources. But just because a book is about an important subject doesn't mean that the book itself is important. It may be incompetent, superficial, too similar to others which covered the ground earlier. The trick for a reviewer is to try to read only those written by authors who speak with some authority and who have something new to say. And that is a harsh criterion. Imagine the difficulty of saying something new and important about race relations or the cold war!

My second point in choosing which books to review is probable literary worth. This, needless to say, is not easy to estimate. But probable good books obviously include new books by authors who have written good books before, writers in whom many readers are certain to be interested: Ernest Hemingway, William Faulkner, Thomas Mann, John P. Marquand, Joyce Cary and many others. Many first novels by unknown authors turn out to be surprisingly good. In fact, a large proportion (perhaps thirty per cent?) of the good novels of any year are first novels. I spend more time worrying about such books than about any other kind.

I read jacket blurbs, and long experience has developed an almost sixth sense by which I judge the publisher's sincerity, whether he actually believes a book is good, or just good enough of its deplorable kind to be popular. I also read the advertising in book trade mgaazines, which often contains clues as to publishers' true opinions of their books. I read the letters publishers write me urging me not to miss the fabulous delights of reading some forthcoming book, discounting some of these letters as worthless examples of crassly commercial enthusiasm and taking a few seriously. And I read sample pages. But I cannot read many sample pages because I lack the time. If I read as many as fifty pages the die is cast. It is too late then to change my mind and try another book. I must go on no matter how uninviting the prospect.

My third point comes up only if neither a book of news value nor one of probable literary worth is available. Then I choose a book which I think will interest me, because I might as well enjoy my work if I can and because I can write a better column about a book which interests me than about one which does not. This indulgence of my own taste is legitimate, I think, and certainly it is one which all critics and reviewers practice whether consciously or not. It explains why in some weeks when no particularly notable book is published, such different books are reviewed. Mr. Jones on one newspaper chooses a book about urban planning. Mr. Smith on another paper chooses one about rock gardens. And I choose a work of history or of historical biography, because, even if it is badly written, its subject matter is certain to interest me. And, to my way of thinking, if a novel is badly written it is beyond redemption.

Sometimes by a sort of divination which includes noting the prickling in my thumbs and watching the flights of pigeons in Times Square, I have premonitions that a book will be poor and know that I must review it anyway; but this is only when the poor book is by a prominent writer and its badness itself is news in the literary world. As a general rule I always try to choose a good book. It is easy to be amusing at the expense of a poor book; but it would be a cheap performance, indeed, deliberately to choose a poor one with the intention of ridiculing it.

There are too many moderately good books available, competent ones if nothing more, which were written in heart's blood with passionate ambition. These may represent years of labor and of hope deferred. If only they were good enough they might bring their author artistic recognition, fame and money—or maybe only the satisfaction of work well done and the comforting knowledge that a few critics recognized good work.

The size of an author's public and the regularity with which his books appear on best-seller charts is no argument that he deserves critical attention. Some of our most popular novelists are mediocre and some are atrociously bad writers. The thousands of happy readers who consume their sub-literary works with innocent relish rarely read book reviews. If they did read one in which their favorite was severely handled they would only be incensed. There would be small use in a critic's regularly denouncing a popular author for his literary crimes and misdemeanors when it is those same offenses which endear him to his public. The critic does better to devote his time and space to books more deserving of critical attention.

The critic's first duty is to his readers. His primary function is to tell them what they want to know about the book in question, to give them enough information and enough opinion so that they can decide whether they wish to read it. In performing this service as best he can, the critic hopes that he can stand up and be counted on the side of the best in writing (according to his feeble lights) and for the best in life itself (according to his fallible judgment). He cares passionately about books. Otherwise he would have gone mad years ago. He likes to write about them. Otherwise he could never face his relentless routine. He hopes that he has been able to do some good service to the cause of a noble art.

Some people try persistently to distract the critic from his true function. Perfectly sincere but wonderfully misguided persons have tried to persuade me that my job is to help sell books and that I should pay particular attention to potentially popular books, rotating my space among the leading publishers. Only thus can I best serve the book business. They look baffled when I insist that I am not employed by the book business, although I wish it well

Vasiliu.

(after all, my own job in the long run depends on it). I am not writing advertising.

Others have argued with me that the critic's duty is to promote deserving writers, to instruct them and teach them and guide them, particularly to do all this for desperately serious authors of ambitious but wretchedly bad books. But the critic is little concerned with good intentions. He is concerned with the book at hand. He wishes aspiring writers well. There are never enough fine books. But readers care much less about ambitious failures than about books which they may wish to read.

The critic must take care to discuss some of the more significant failures, some of the unsuccessful experiments, some of the pretentious novels which don't come off. He must do so because sometimes these are written by new writers of major talent and promise; and because such books are often interesting in spite of their egregious faults. They often show which way the winds of literary doctrine are blowing.

Soon after I began writing daily book columns for *The New York Times* I discovered that it was impossible to get my work done if I went to the office every day. There were too many distractions and interruptions there, books to sort, telephone calls and correspondence to answer, callers to see. All this consumed so much time that there wasn't enough left for reading and writing. So I adopted a schedule which takes me to the city three times a week, on Mondays, Wednesdays and Fridays. On Tuesdays, Thursdays and Saturdays I stay home and work in my library. Six full-time working days a week, however, are not enough. I always spend several hours several evenings a week reading what my children used to call "work books."

On my city days I try to finish my various odd jobs in

time to begin serious reading before lunch, but often don't succeed. I read all afternoon and all the way home on the commuting train. On home days I begin reading before eight o'clock and read all day with only a half-hour out for lunch. If I am reading a book of reasonable length I usually can start writing at about four o'clock. Long books which require several days to read throw me all out of schedule and increase the number of evenings spent at work. Two hours is usually enough in which to write a column. It generally works out that I write three columns at home and one in the office each week.

Compared with most people I am a moderately fast reader. Compared with most people professionally occupied in the world of books I am a slow reader. My daughter when she was only sixteen could read half again as fast as I and remember what she read in impressive detail. How she does it I don't know and neither does she. Perhaps young people today are taught to read differently. I learned that c-a-t spells cat. Jennifer and all her generation, if I understand it aright, learned that the three letters "c" and "a" and "t" when lumped together mean cat, looking at the three letters as a group and not separately. Of course, that is what we all get in the habit of doing with familiar words. We don't read all the letters in them. But the young seem to get the hang of it much more efficiently. And really fast readers read several words at a time by a sort of visual trick which enables them to grasp the meaning, but which eliminates any possibility of appreciating the style.

Even though I must rely on comparatively horse-and-buggy reading methods, I have learned that speed in reading can be increased substantially by mere effort, by concentrating on reading as fast as possible. It can also be increased astronomically by skipping. Many people who claim to be exceptionally rapid readers are unconscious skippers. They fool themselves and don't realize how much they have skipped.

Skipping, I think, is completely justified if the book is bad. But who, except a professional critic, reads a book he believes is bad? If the book is good, skipping is inexcusable. And only a little less culpable is reading in word groups. Both time-saving tricks are absolutely unfair to the author. They sabotage his means of communication. They destroy the emotional quality of the words the author chose and of the order in which he arranged them—which is style. And style depends on hearing the sound of the words with the inner ear. If one doesn't hear the rhythms and verbal music of the words, if one doesn't almost taste their flavor and feel their texture, one might as well read Gibbon rewritten by Walter Winchell, Shakespeare, mutilated for comic book readers.

The art of reading requires the use of two senses, not one. The eye must take in and the ear must hear. The ear will normally disconnect itself if the words the eye is looking at are poorly chosen. But if a reader has any appreciation of language and poetry and beauty, his ear will tune in when he reads good writing. If the author had any serious aspirations toward art and was not just trying to earn an honest penny by hack work, he chose his words with care and arranged them with prayer. Other words and other arrangements would not do. They would not sound right. The ones he chose sound as nearly right as he could make them.

Reading, of course, does not make demands only on the eye and ear. It requires the active use of the whole mind. Reading can be a passive enjoyment, a soothing distraction, like smoking opium. But at its best it is an active exercise of the intellect and the imagination, and also of the emotions. To read fine books without feeling sympathy, grief, joy, love and indignation is to miss the richest part of the reading experience. To be a good reader requires concentrated effort, whole-hearted cooperation with the author. It cannot be done with a lazy mind and an indifferent spirit.

A critic's reading is always done against time. The inexorable deadlines when reviews must be turned in to the copy desk are like hurdles in an obstacle race, but a race with no end. As soon as one is crossed, the next is upon you. Calendars and clocks rule your life. You always know what the date is, for it is publication day of such-and-such which was scheduled for the tenth; and what time it is, for three o'clock leaves one more hour to read the last seventy pages and two hours in which to write a review. It is nice to stop work at six if possible and read the morning newspaper, which most people read ten hours earlier. Surely in few other professions do you so regularly hear time's winged chariot hurrying near. You watch with dismay that 900-page opus on the crisis of Western man rolling on like Juggernaut itself; and knowing that you cannot read even a decent two-thirds of it in two days, you devote three evenings to it in advance, evenings when it might be considerably more fun to go to the movies, or to play Scrabble, or to listen to Brahms.

Some people think that a literary critic leads a leisurely life, that all he does is curl up with a good book and then toss off a few brilliant remarks about it which are quoted at all the best cocktail parties. They think that he lunches regularly with beautiful young authors of sensational best sellers, that he is frequently flattered by distinguished publishers. It looks so easy, an overstuffed chair, a pipe and probably a nap after lunch. This misconception was succinctly expressed by my son some years ago when he was very young, but even then he should have known better: "When I grow up, I want to be a book reviewer like Daddy, so I can sit down all day."

An even more astonishing notion of the way a critic works is one which I encounter several times a year: "Do you really read all those books? You must have an assistant who does most of the reading and you just do the writing." Once you have choked down the contemptuous and explosive answer such a question deserves, you can only reply with weary resignation: "How could I know what I thought of a book if I didn't read it? My job isn't to write other people's opinions." The idea of other people doing the critic's reading for him sounds so preposterous that I can hardly expect anyone to believe how many otherwise sane people hold it.

A few years ago I looked up from my office desk one bright day in June and there before me was as attractive a girl as ever graduated from Vassar. This pretty young lady had done just that the previous week and was anxious to begin a career as a literary critic. She was willing to start, she admitted modestly, as my assistant and wouldn't expect payment. She would make life easier for me by reading books and telling me all about them and then I could write the reviews without having overly exerted myself. Or, if I preferred, she would read the books and write the reviews herself and all I would have to do would be to sign my name to them!

Pretty but addle-pated girls aren't the only callers who find their way to my well-concealed office at the *Times*. Publishers' publicity men and women (most of them welcome because they are nice people) drop in just to make sure that none of the wonderful books on their lists are overlooked. Struggling authors often present themselves. Usually they are young and usually they are unpublished. They want me to read their manuscripts, make editorial suggestions (probably unnecessary) and recommend them to publishers.

Authors of published books come, too, but never well-established ones. They demand to know why their books were not reviewed when other books not nearly so good were. The basic reason is that other books seemed more promising. But the cruel truth must be put gently, and the competition for space is stressed with sweeping gestures toward our overflowing book cases.

Other callers come only to denounce my deplorable opinions, to ask me to join something, to leave autographed copies of books which they had privately printed at their own expense. They know that there are lots of books published, but they will be watching the *Times* for a review of theirs. Copies may be had by calling in person at the author's home.

More dramatic and unpredictable than my callers is my mail. The fan letters are always pleasing, even when I suspect that they are written by jugheads. The angry, bitter, sarcastic, sneering, insulting, scurrilous and obscene letters of abuse are sometimes amusing; but often it is more than I can manage to be amused by them. They are too exasperating. Many of these are anonymous. Many of them are written by near-illiterates and these always make me speculate how such benighted souls came to be reading book reviews in the first place. They have accused me of being a communist and a fascist (I am a lukewarm Republican), an enemy of literature and a champion of pornography (because I saw some merit in a moderately realistic novel). Many letters are warm, chatty, friendly and personal, obviously written by people who read the "Books of The Times" column regularly and are lonely and have plenty of leisure in which to write. And some letters are written by cranks and crackpots, who have nothing better to do than air their follies and obsessions in letters to the papers.

In moments of humility I remind myself that there is always the possibility that some of the letters which seem to me to be abusive nonsense might not seem so to others. They might think them trenchant criticisms of my short-comings. Maybe the scornful correspondent who called me "a muddled hypocrite" was denouncing me for my own good. But I can't think that the gentleman who wrote me four letters in two weeks accusing me of being "a tool of Moscow" and of being "a cheap unchristian dog, of no experience or feeling" was writing in a spirit of judicious calm.

More fun to read was the letter from an admirer who expressed his restrained approval as follows: "I can find only one word for your work and yourself, 'hypsilophron,' from the Greek hypsilos, high, and phrono, thinking and contemplating. The word may be translated as lofty thinker and observer of values. Or I may say that I find in your work a perfect justification of the meaning of your first name from the French *or,* for gold, and *ville,* for city—a gold city or a gold mine of wisdom and character." One can't count on getting a letter like that every day.

And what were the intentions of the woman who wrote to me as follows? "I am a woman, a daughter of Eve and not of the gods. Surely we may be forgiven for comforting each other when we were both lost in the desert—but now

I have found my certainty again. I know the way out but I am loath to go alone. Nevertheless I shall if I cannot persuade you—for I was born free, and free I have ever been. And were you not also? How foolish then for us to permit the salacious imaginations of small minds to fasten the yoke of immorality upon us! To protest would be folly—but to act as if it were so is a crime against ourselves and God." This was so sudden.

And my favorite letter of all, which came from a European capital:

"Dear Mr. Prescott:

Through the kindness of friends I have received and receive still regularly *The New York Times*. In this paper I read frequently your criticism of books.

"I should have said that I am a doktor, what is called Psycho Analist in the modern world, the name has taken on sinister meaning and I prefer to be addressed just as Doktor. I am a refugee from Vienna, and I wear a beard, ecco the perfect P.A.

"I have often doubted the good we can do, and although I am in great need of money I say no, several times a year to cases that seem hopeless to me. But I think I can help you.

"Through reading your reviews over a period of years, I have diagnosed your trouble, that is, it needs no diagnosis; it is obvious to the ordinary person of perception that you suffer and most probably you are the one who does not know it and I offer to cure you.

"I think that your case is easily straightened out, as it is manifesting herself in your writings; it is an elementary case; you are not burdened with—well, in this letter I will not go too far in explaining and take your valuable time. I will arrive in New York, and write you again, for an appointment when we can discuss this further."

I never heard further from the good doctor, but I still wonder after seven years if his letter was a hoax. I prefer to think that it was. But maybe— Oh, my!

To write daily book reviews for a great newspaper is to occupy an exposed position in the front rank during the unceasing battle of the books. It also means that one's adult education is continually going on in a glass class-room. One's private opinions are public property and one's most sacred convictions are stripped naked for the world to stare at. Necessarily, one makes many enemies, authors of books reviewed unfavorably or not reviewed at all, their friends and relations, readers who disagree with one's literary beliefs, or readers who despise one's political, social and moral philosophy. Necessarily also, one makes friends, authors one praises with singularly discriminating perception, their friends and relations, readers who agree and approve. But, save for the comparatively few letter writers, friends and enemies remain unknown.

To write daily book reviews for a great newspaper is a pleasure and a privilege and a source of joyful excite-ment. It means that one is constantly in the company, through the written word, of sensitive, observant, thought-ful, intelligent and interesting men and women; that one is always learning about people and ideas and events and issues; that one is a charter member of that great brother-hood of men and women who think that the writing and reading of books is one of the most important and certainly the most truly civilized of all human activities.

And, most exciting of all, to write book reviews for a great newspaper is to exercise a sobering responsibility.

One can call the attention of a not inconsiderable body of readers to the books one sincerely admires. One can know the intense joy of discovery and the pleasure of sharing that discovery with others. Occasionally one can serve as a literary herald and blow a trumpet at the gates of the city of educated men and women announcing the arrival of books which, in one's humble but firmly held opinion, deserve to become part of our enduring culture. And one can also champion the essential ideas and the permanent standards which must be preserved if our culture is to remain worth preserving.

The individual critic's influence is limited and often offset by that of other critics of contrary mind. He, like all other men, is a product of his times and cannot influence them much. But he can do his utmost to see that such influence as he has is thrown on the right side of the scales, on the side of good books and of the good life, on the side of freedom and honor and self-respect and love and individual responsibility.

·*fifteen*·

Sunday afternoon, December 7, 1941, Lilias and I took the children for a walk in the fields and woods near the house we were renting on Carter Street. When we got back to the house it was too late to hear the regular broadcast of the New York Philharmonic Symphony Orchestra, and so we did not turn on the radio until nearly nine o'clock in the evening. It was only then that we heard the news of the Japanese attack on Pearl Harbor.

That the United States would be involved in the war against Hitler, I had been long convinced. I thought also that we ought to be. But this was so unexpected that I felt dazed with a sort of combined intellectual and emotional shock. And it was while still suffering from that condition that I delivered a lecture the following afternoon, Monday, December eighth, to a women's club in Providence. The proceedings seemed gruesome and revolting. On such a day who cared about the current books and what I thought about them?

During the next few months, while the bad news multiplied and our country geared itself for war, I, like a million others, debated what my own proper course of action should be. If I had been ten years younger or ten years older, there would have been no problem. But I was in my thirty-sixth year. I was the father of two children. I was a literary critic and such special skills as I had were not of urgent importance to the war effort.

After much painful self-examination I decided that I would volunteer if I could get a commission, as so many other men of my generation were doing, but that if I could not get a commission I would wait to be drafted. During the next few months I applied for a commission or a chance to attend an officers' training school at four different departments of the Navy. In one of them the young officer who interviewed me almost sneered when he learned what my profession was. With considerable sarcasm he inquired whether I knew anything useful, like electrical engineering, arc welding or radio repairing. I had to plead ignorance and was dismissed. The Navy, even in its communication and publicity departments, had no need of literary critics. This rebuff was irritating. But I was considerably more irritated a few days later when a friend told me about a friend of his who had just received his commission in the Navy. Since he was a designer of women's dresses it was not easy to see how he could be more useful than a literary critic.

I was still brooding on this situation when the *Times* job was offered to me in March, 1942. That settled it. The decision from then on was up to my draft board. I spent the next three years waiting for a call which never came. During that time I estimated that nearly half of the books I wrote about were concerned with some aspect of the war. More than half of every lecture I delivered was devoted to the war, also. I rode a bicycle to the station to save gasoline and watched the night-time skies for enemy airplanes. But all I know about modern war, like most of what I know about everything else, I learned from printed words.

When I went to the airplane observation post for my turn on the two to four A.M. shift one Saturday night in the first week of July, 1943, I did not foresee anything of particular importance to me. My usual partner was unable to come that morning and I found a stranger in his place. While we watched the sky for German bombers and reported by telephone the passing of the regular New York to Boston plane, we helped each other keep awake by desultory conversation.

John, it soon appeared, was depressed by the fact that after a whole year he was still unable to sell a house from which he had been forced to move by unexpected increases in the size of his family. It was a nice house, nine rooms, paneled dining room, modern kitchen, a semi-basement room left unfinished which would make an ideal play-room, study or library.

I hadn't been paying much attention. Three A.M. is not my best time. But when he mentioned that potential library I was suddenly intensely interested. It was just what I needed. In fact, the whole house sounded ideal for my family. As my interest became apparent, John's celebrated salesmanship was turned on full force. By the time our relief arrived at four I had arranged to bring Lilias to see the house at eleven the next morning, or rather that morning.

My interest flared up so quickly because I was then engaged in negotiations to buy the house which we had rented for nearly four years. It was comfortable and pleasantly located. But it was old without being quaint. Its furnace burned coal, it needed many repairs and improve-

ments, and it was considerably larger than was sensible for us. I thought a low price was in order.

The owner's idea of a low price was so far above mine that the possibility of a meeting of minds seemed remote indeed. Nevertheless, he wanted to sell the house to somebody if not to me. He was tired of renting it. The night I met John I had decided that it was high time I did something constructive about the future shelter of the Prescott family. When I went back to bed a little after four I said to Lilias, "I've just bought a house I've never seen." She was less than half awake at the time, but that slight exaggeration woke her up beautifully.

At eleven o'clock Sunday morning we went to look at the house. It was everything John said it was, not a gem of architecture, but an attractive combination of white clapboard and gray shingles. Set well back from the road on rather a steep hill, it was surrounded by oak and dogwood trees. And the semi-basement study was perfect for my needs. Because it was in the basement, earth came nearly halfway up its outer walls. But because of the slope of the ground it had windows on three sides. There was plenty of room for book shelves.

An hour after Lilias and I first set eyes on the house I handed John the sum of one dollar as an option on the house, good until the following night. I needed that much time to consider the finances involved. Fortunately for me, the great real estate boom, which sent prices soaring in our town and in a thousand others within the next year, had not yet begun. John's price was reasonable and soon the house was ours.

We have never regretted our decision. This is our home. Here our children have grown up. Here we have known great happiness and some of the anxieties and griefs which come to all mortals, terrifying illness and news of the deaths of those we loved. This is where we have done much of our best living.

Our little garden is pretty because Lilias has worked hard with little help from me to make it so. The living room and my library are filled with books, not only because I work with them, but because all four of us love books. Many of them are great or greatly beloved books which I read for the second or third time when reading aloud to the children. Some of them are books which I read as a child, which the children read when they were little and which they have put aside for their children when the proper time comes.

From my library windows I have looked out over my temporarily stalled typewriter and watched bluebirds, swallows and robins. Every spring I can admire dogwood blossoms foaming near the windows. In the summer peonies bloom and in the autumn chrysanthemums. Sitting here in the same chair beside the same desk which used to be in my room in the Fairmount Boulevard house, I have written several million words. The *Cue* column continued until 1947. For six years, from 1943 through 1949, I wrote the fiction reviews of *The Yale Review*. For several years I wrote the book reviews for a California magazine. And now two books have been written here. There will, I hope, be others. There would have been already if the time for writing books did not have to be snatched from my so-called leisure.

Some people think that houses acquire personalities of their own, soaked up from the people who have lived in them and all the emotions which have been felt within their walls. That this is possible I doubt, but if it were, ours should be a happy house. We have had our problems and troubles, but our problems and troubles have been minor compared with those which are the lot of many. We are grateful for good fortune. But we are proud, too, of the success we believe that we have made of being a family. Always all four of us have enjoyed doing many things together, from going to the movies to going to Europe. And nearly always, with due allowance made for inevitable lapses into human pettishness, we have tried to make our lives a demonstration of the fact that we do love each other.

In this, our psychopathically self-conscious age of tension and fear, we continually hear confused and confusing talk about love. Psychiatrists insist that children need the warm security of being loved, a truth which all good parents have always known. Hack writers of self-help books and sincere preachers of the word of God exhort us to love one another and thereby help not only others but ourselves. Their exhortations are based upon a great truth. The world would certainly be better off with more love in it. But it is hard to love the human race. Most of us have to make a humbler start by loving a few humans. And many people who protest most loudly that they love mankind seem heartily to dislike an astonishing proportion of the individual men and women of their acquaintance.

Even when love is discussed on an individual basis, it is often discussed in its most limited or even in its basest manifestations. I have read in books and have heard people talk as if love were identical with sexual passion. Since the sexual instinct is a bodily impulse not always dependent on emotion, this is absurd. Sex can be an expression of love, but it is not love itself.

True love between men and women, I do most fervently believe, includes many other factors of which the most important are spontaneous joy in the other's company, a loyal partnership in the whole experience of living and, perhaps most important of all, a complete and daily dedication to the other's happiness and welfare.

Believing as I do in such a concept of love between men and women, believing also that my life has been infinitely enriched by such a love, I often look with wonder and alarm at the marriages I encounter in life and in books. In both I have met many obviously happily married people. But so many others seem to marry when they do not even really like each other, when they have no community of interests and no commonly held basic convictions. Many marriages which cannot be dismissed as unhappy still seem to be only workable compromises with no element of joy or beauty. And all too many are only temporary arrangements for convenience in mating, with their termination in the divorce court fully foreseen by both parties to the fraudulent contract.

Love of children, as Solomon knew so well, is one of the most powerful of human emotions. All parents don't share it, some being too selfish and self-absorbed. But as a general rule it is a wonderfully effective contribution to the enduring strength of marriage. But children grow older and need their parents' love and guidance less and less. They soon become individual human beings subject to their share of the handicaps of fate, heredity and environment, but responsible in the long run for their own virtues and sins and their own actions. When that time comes, as it nearly has for our children, all the parents can do is take comfort in the thought that they have done their best and recognize the fact that for good or ill their own journey is much more than half completed.

We, all parents of nearly grown children, have grown

up ourselves as best we could (never an easy task). We have helped our children as best we could and at the same time we have lived through the best years of our maturity. There remains only the prospect, pleasant or unpleasant according to your philosophy, of growing old as gracefully as possible.

How to do that in the shadow of the hydrogen bomb! If we only knew. Many smug and officious people claim that they know how, and offer to tell us for a reasonable admission fee. You must have faith, they exclaim, as if faith were something that one could put on like heavy underwear in winter. Faith in what? In the future? In the wisdom and benevolence of the Kremlin Politburo? In the religious doctrines of the person speaking?

More irritating are the false prophets who try to dismiss our well-founded fears as if they were mere trifles, and frighten us instead with fear of getting fat, or old, or of falling behind the Joneses. Their motives are cynically commercial and their opinions of the human race are sickeningly low. They contribute to the successful functioning of our economy by appealing to the least worthy motives of men, to vanity, snobbery, jealousy and greed. They make us want so much we do not need and so much else that we don't even truly want. Such false prophets can sometimes be ignored by an effort of will. We cannot ignore the crisis of civilization in which we live.

That the crisis is not only the conflict between totalitarian states allied with or conquered by Communist Russia and the free states of the world ought to be obvious. That conflict is crucial and probably will not be settled in our time. It may break out in war so horrible that the few survivors will not consider themselves lucky. It may only simmer, with little wars and small-scale crises.

All this would be easier to face if Western men were united in their beliefs and confident about the health of their civilization. Since they are not, ours is far more truly a time which tries men's souls than that of which Tom Paine wrote. It is difficult to live in such a time without cultivating all manner of fears and obsessions. But it is not impossible to call on our reserves of intelligence, reason and patience and to live with at least a decent minimum of grace.

Always we can act as if we had more courage than in our inmost thoughts we suspect we actually have. We can each do his little best to aid the cause of freedom. We can stand up and be counted on what we believe to be the side of righteousness. We can try to understand the issues and forces and circumstances which beset our poor, tormented world. And after we have informed ourselves as best we can and taken what little positive action we can (and precious little it is), we can stop talking about catastrophe for more than a strictly rationed interval each day.

There are some things we can't do a thing about. We are not the only generation which has felt sorry for itself. Death and disaster have always lurked around the corner. Michel Eyquem Seigneur de Montaigne, one of the wisest men who ever lived, felt much the same way in the sixteenth century as we do today and remained calm. "Who is there," he wrote, "that, seeing our civil wars, does not cry out that this machine, the world, is being overthrown and that the day of judgment is seizing us by the throat without calling to mind that many worse things have happened, and that, notwithstanding, ten thousand parts of the world are meanwhile having a merry time?"

It is wise, I think, to remember that although public opinion is a force which men of might must reckon with, and our opinion is part of public opinion, still the terrifying decisions for life and death will not be made by us, but by a few men with power. We can only wait and hope and pray that they will make their decisions wisely. We shall have no reason to be surprised if they don't.

Wisdom is a rare seasoning in the vast stew of human affairs. It has never been the meat and potatoes. If the hydrogen bombs fall, the horror will be unimaginable. But they may not fall until next week, next month or next year. In the meantime we can go about our daily business. We can continue to love our dear ones and to lead the good life to the best of our ability. The bombs have been with us for more than ten years. During those years wise men and women did not live in panic. They found much to enjoy in life. Life is to be lived, not to be spent cowering before a dreadful possibility.

In 1947 I shared a seat on the commuting train with a distinguished friend of mine, a writer and lecturer on international problems, who greeted me as I sat down beside him with a question: "Do you realize that you have only two more years to live?" He had it all worked out, the atom bombs multiplied by his sure knowledge of the secret decisions of the Comintern divided by the width of the Atlantic Ocean. As I write this in 1955 he is already more than six years wrong. It is possible that he may be wrong by fifty or a hundred years. No one knows. But, it seems to me, the only reasonable way for reasonable beings to live is as if he were wrong by many years. If he is wrong by only a few years, we shall still have spent them well.

In a world shattered by war, paralyzed by fear, rent by social, political, and spiritual change, it is impossible for well-informed people to be "cockeyed optimists," like Ensign Nellie Forbush of *South Pacific*. But it is possible to be pessimistic calmly, to refuse to have hysterics over things we can't help, to enjoy the good things and the good experiences of life while there are any.

The fragrance of the lilacs which bloom outside my study window each spring is just as lovely as that of the lilacs which bloomed in poets' dooryards a hundred years ago. New peas taste just as good in the age of anxiety as they did in the gay nineties. The great books have lost nothing of their greatness. Children are just as exasperating and just as enchanting as they were when the Reverend Charles Lutwidge Dodgson told stories to a little girl in Oxford. Love is the same exquisite, terrifying and ennobling emotion it has always been. And to live in these darkling and portentous times, so filled with interest and excitement, is an even greater adventure than to live in less eventful periods.

Those of us who are middle-aged or older have seen the world change almost beyond recognition. We have seen horrors unspeakable; but so far we have survived them, and most of us in this fortunate country have had little or limited contact with them. We should be grateful for our blessings. And if in the blackness of the night we fear that our children will not be so fortunate as we, why, then, it behooves us all the more to do our utmost to make their lives and those of all their generation as rich as possible with love and happiness, with knowledge and courage, so that they may know something of the joy of life even as we did—if only briefly—so that they will be equipped as well as possible to face whatever the future holds.

ABOUT THE AUTHOR

ORVILLE PRESCOTT has been known to call himself a typical New Yorker—because he comes from the Middle West, lived in New York for only six years and then moved to Connecticut. Since 1942 his daily book reviews have appeared in *The New York Times*. A native of Cleveland, a graduate of Williams, the husband of a Smith alumna and the father of a Harvard son and a Radcliffe daughter, he has written for magazines and newspapers all his adult life. His book of literary criticism, *In My Opinion: An Inquiry into the Contemporary Novel,* delighted many readers and outraged others, a response which could easily have been predicted by anyone familiar with his spirited, forthright and controversial *Times* reviews.